It's All About God

To Thomas
God Bless You
Jesus Loves You

It's All About God

Demetrice Gates

KNB Publications, LLC
http://www.knb-publications.com

KNB titles are published by:

KNB Publications, LLC
P.O. Box 831648
Stone Mountain, GA 30083
Email: info@knb-publications.com

Copyright © 2008 by Demetrice Gates

All rights reserved. No part of this book may be reproduced, stored in retrieval system, or transmitted in any form or by any means without the prior written consent of the Publisher, except in the case of brief quotations embodied in critical articles or reviews.

KNB Publications, LLC is a Christian Book Publisher dedicated to expanding works that uplift Jesus Christ through the written word. The KNB logo is a registered trademark.

ISBN 10: 0-9789702-8-4
ISBN 13: 978-0-9789702-8-4

First Printing: November 2008

Printed in the United States of America

TABLE OF CONTENTS

INTROLOVETION

MISSION POSSIBLE

CHAPTER 1: INSPIRATIONAL

CHAPTER 2: MOTIVATIONAL

CHAPTER 3: ENCOURAGING

ABOUT THE AUTHOR

INTROLOVETION

Give unto the Lord the glory due unto his name; worship the Lord in the beauty of holiness (Psalm 29:2). Everything about the Lord is beautiful. His love for you is beautiful, my brothers and sisters. At this very moment, He is thinking about you. He will always keep you in His heart. Know that it's all about God, and do not forget about Him. May peace be with you, and God bless you.

MISSION POSSIBLE

First of all, let me say I love God Almighty. He is my Heavenly Father. I'm still supposed to be in heaven with Him, but He called me to this special mission for Him. Before I came to earth, God had a conversation with me. I forgot what name He called me, but it means warrior. I told God I was willing to do anything He asked me to do. The other servants didn't want to leave heaven because it is so glorious. Satan knew that I was on my way down to earth. God had sent me to this planet as fast as I could get here. That's the reason why I was born legs first; so that the doctors could pull me out of my mother's womb as quickly as possible.

Before God sent me to earth, He told me that He had equipped my body so I would be able to take punishment because Satan was going to try his best to destroy me. This explains why I went through so much, both as a child and young adult. I got hit by a truck, a baseball bat, I slipped into a brick wall, my legs were broken and injured again as the result of a weight lifting accident, I have had multiple surgeries, and the enemy tried to take my mind as well. But you know what my brothers and sisters? I'm still living and standing. While I was in heaven, I asked God to put me in a family that would strongly support me. He showed me the future of this family. The family that He put me in is going to help tear down the kingdom of Satan. This family is going to pull a lot of souls in to God.

I'm what you call a time traveler for God, in the spiritual sense; a visionary, like the Prophet Ezekiel. I was with David when he wrote Psalms. I was with Solomon when he wrote Proverbs. I was also with Paul. That explains why I'm a writer for the Kingdom of God. God showed me the marvelous works that He is going to do for this family. He is so powerful! He said it's time to stop playing games. It's time to cut the evil doers' heads off with the sword of the Spirit. God said let us start having order in the church for His Son is coming back soon. We all know who His Son is; He is the great Jesus Christ. He showed me the church that our family is going to have. It is going to be huge. Gay people are going to attend; prostitutes, and all of the above; but once they get saved and delivered, they are going to be a part of the greatest family ever created, the family of Christ.

Chapter One

INSPIRATIONAL

A TRUE FRIEND

I love God; He is so special to me. Whenever I call on Him, He's always there to answer me. God is a Lord of hope. He is a God of many great wonders, but most of all, a true friend.

Have mercy upon me, O Lord; for I am weak: O Lord, heal me; for my bones are vexed (Psalm 6:2). Whenever I'm weak, God will be there to make me strong. When I'm sick, He's my remedy. He will heal me from anything. God told me all I have to do is believe in Him, and accept His Son, Jesus Christ, as my personal Savior. God is real; He's in my everyday life.

I will both lay me down in peace, and sleep: for thou, Lord, only makes me dwell in safety (Psalm 4:8). The only time I feel peace is when I'm in the presence of God. The Lord is my bodyguard; He will protect me from anything, especially the evil forces of Satan. He won't allow evil to get near me. Whenever evil approaches, God will quickly destroy it because He is a powerful force. I take our relationship seriously because I love God, and He loves me.

I will praise thee, O Lord, with my whole heart; I will show forth all thy marvelous works (Psalm 9:1). As long as I live, I will continue to praise God. I will continue to spread His great name at any place I go. Whenever I'm lonely, He's always there to keep me company. What many people need to realize, is that God has enough love to go around because He is a true friend to live in peace with.

A TRUE HERO

I love the Lord because He is constantly in my life. Everyday, the Lord smiles down on all of His children. The Lord is a true hero; He gave David the strength to defeat Goliath, and He gave Noah a design for how He wanted him to build the ark. God is not a comic book or action movie hero, but a real hero. *Though I walk in the midst of trouble, thou wilt revive me: thou shalt stretch forth thine hand against the wrath of mine enemies, and thy right hand shall save me* (Psalm 138:7). There is no situation or trouble too big that God cannot handle. God will help you with all of your problems. He will bring you out of your suffering. When the disciples started to lose faith, and Jesus saw the storm and the fear in His disciples, He spoke to the winds and the sea and there was a great calm (Matthew 8:23-27). God is powerful and a strong force in the day of trouble.

In our sorrows, He will be there to comfort us. When we lose hope, He will be our confidence. *My flesh and my heart faileth: but God is the strength of my heart, and my portion forever* (Psalm 73:26). The closer you get to God, the more trouble Satan is going to try to put you through. I'd rather be with God and go through trials, and tribulations than to be with Satan and go to hell.

At the end, the children of God are going to rejoice in His holy name. We know that the Almighty God has something great in store for us. That's why it's worth going through trials and tribulations, because at the end, God will be victorious, and the true hero will be standing.

BE A SOLDIER

Sometimes, God gets sick and tired of people crying and complaining all the time. He says to Himself, "Why do they have so little faith?" In John 16:33, Jesus said, *In the world ye shall have tribulation.* Jesus is telling us while we are in this world, we are going to go through tribulations and hard times because we are not of the world. God is telling me to tell you to be a soldier.

Don't get me wrong, I used to cry all the time. I also had little faith; but once you give God your whole heart, mind, body, and soul, the crying should stop because you are saved. The Lord doesn't want anyone dropping tears unless they are tears of joy. God doesn't put sorrow in your heart, He puts joy in it.

When you are going through a tribulation, hold on to God and be tough. God doesn't want any cowards in His army, He wants soldiers. If you can't have faith in God through your tribulations, what are you going to do when the war between good and evil really breaks out? You have to put all your faith and trust in God. Don't let your mind be wavering.

To all of my friends: stand strong in the midst of your tribulations. Be like Job and be patient. Always remember that God is on your side. It is important for us to take back our children from Satan. We have to raise our children the way God wants us to, so hold on to your faith and be a soldier.

BE STRONG

One thing I try my best to be is strong. Being strong is the key to success. When you are strong, nothing can stop you from reaching your goals. No, I'm not talking about lifting weights or exercising, but having a strong spirit.

First of all, to be strong you have to have faith in God. God will bless you to be so strong that you will break down any wall. *The righteous also shall hold on his way, and he that hath clean hands shall be stronger and stronger* (Job 17:9). When you are spiritually strong, you can fight through any temptation. Things will also become easy for you. *I can do all things through Christ which strengtheneth me.* (Philippians 4:13) All of us have to believe in Christ, and have faith in Him, that nothing is impossible for Him.

Moreover, you've got to have courage. Don't fear anyone, or anything, but God. God doesn't want any of us to be weak; He wants us to be strong in Him. *Lord, by thy favor thou hast made my mountain to stand strong: thou didst hide thy face, and I was troubled* (Psalm 30:7). When you are strong in God, you are automatically strong in yourself because He is in you. Let God control your heart, mind, and soul because He will lead you the right way. *Wait on the Lord: be of good courage and he shall strengthen thine heart: wait, I say on the Lord* (Psalm 27:14).

DO YOU TRULY LOVE GOD?

Let me ask you a question. Do you truly love God? If you do, you will bless Him everyday. You will tell others how marvelous He is. You will share of His goodness with others. God truly loves you. He takes care of you everyday. He takes care of your worries. Worship God on a daily basis. Praise His holy name any place that you travel.

O give thanks unto the Lord; for he is good: for his mercy endureth for ever (Psalm 118:29). God gives all of us mercy. He knows that it is difficult to live in a world of sin. That's why I love God; because He understands everything that goes on down here on earth. Many people say that they love God, but they don't mean it. They are the biggest hypocrites in the world. They preach to other people about living like Christ, but their own lives neither honor nor reflect Him. If you truly love God, you won't deceive others. If you do, believe me, you are going to pay for it. God is not someone to play with, which means that He is a force that can and will destroy you.

My brothers and sisters, I want you to dwell with God. Show God love just like He shows you love. Be willing to bless Him. Be willing to serve Him. He will be happy to reward you. Before the world began, God prepared the kingdom for His children. You can be part of that if you would just believe and trust in Him. Give God all your love. He's already given you all of His.

DON'T WORRY ABOUT YOUR ENEMIES

How are you doing, my brothers and sisters? I hope you all are doing great. I'm feeling just fine. It feels so good to have the grace of God, knowing He is our Father. My brothers and sisters, you don't have to worry about your enemies because God will handle them.

Through God we shall do valiantly: for he it is that shall tread down our enemies (Psalm 60:12). All God wants us to be is brave. He does not want us to be weak. God will not let your enemies touch you. It is He who shields and protects you when you are walking in the valley of death. Continue to walk toward God as though nothing will stop you.

That he would grant unto us, that we, being delivered out of the hand of our enemies, might serve him without fear (Luke 1:74). God wants all of us to serve Him without fear *because he had not given us the spirit of fear; but of power, and of love, and of a sound mind* (2 Timothy 1:7). God will deliver you from anything. He will deliver you from drugs, alcohol, smoking, and from your enemies. Serve God with all your strength. Shout out His name even when your throat hurts. God deserves all of your attention. He deserves all of your time.

My brothers and sisters, God has a special place for us. He's getting all of us prepared for it. Any trial that you go through, count it all as joy. God is trying to strengthen you. He never fails at doing His job. He is a God of perfection. Just remember that God always has your back, so don't worry about your enemies.

DON'T BE AFRAID

Hello. How are you doing? I'm writing this paper to tell you don't be afraid. Many of us say we are not afraid, but the truth is, we are. There is no reason to be fearful because the Lord is with you. I used to be afraid too, but when I got strong in the Lord, the spirit of fear went away; *for God had not given us the spirit of fear; but of power, and of love, and of a sound mind* (2 Timothy 1:7).

God is our refuge and strength, a very present help in trouble (Psalm 46:1). The Lord will be there to protect you from any danger. He won't let anything hurt or harm you. Wherever you go, just remember the Lord will be there. God is your protector and bodyguard. He will always be there to help you in time of need.

Yea, thou I walk through the valley of the shadow of death, I will fear no evil: for thou art with me; thy rod and thy staff they comfort me (Psalm 23:4). The Lord is your rod and staff. He will destroy any evil that approaches you. Just like a tornado, God will sweep over your enemies. He won't leave any evil behind for the rescue team to find because the Lord doesn't leave trouble behind.

My dear friends, always remember that the Lord is your knight in shining armor. With His sword, He will utterly destroy all of your enemies. God doesn't want you to fear any man or any thing, *so that we may boldly say, the Lord is my helper, and I will not fear what man shall do unto me* (Hebrews 13:6). And on that note, my friends, don't be afraid.

GENTLE SPIRIT

You know the Lord loves those who are humble. Like Him, a person who is humble is slow to anger. A person who is humble also has a gentle spirit. When you have a gentle spirit, people love to be around you. They feel peace when they are in your presence. People also feel that they can talk to you about anything, even their problems.

First of all, be just like the Almighty God. When people need you, don't turn your back on them. The Lord is always there for His children whenever they cry out for Him. Just like a pillow, the Lord is a comforter for all of His children. His voice is so gentle that it can calm a ferocious beast.

God will comfort your hearts, and stablish you in every good word and work (2 Thessalonians 2:17). No matter what people say or do to you, don't make them feel bad. It's not good to hold grudges. Do less arguing and more compromising, because fussing and fighting doesn't help a relationship grow. Let God be the mediator of your household.

In the world today, we need more people with gentle spirits. The violence in this world is constantly growing. I'm praying that everyone accepts Jesus Christ as his or her personal Savior, because He is the sole provider of a gentle spirit.

GOD IS IN CONTROL

It feels so good to be shielded by God. A marvelous God is He. He does all He can to provide for His children. God never leaves His children starving. My brothers and sisters, don't worry about your life, for God is in control.

When God is in control, everything runs smoothly, even when you are going through hell. You should just relax, and let God handle His business. God will build you into a powerful soldier. Demons will be afraid to go near you. All God wants you to do is serve Him.

When God is in control, you don't have to worry about anything. He will help you pay your bills. He will give you the house you desire. He will provide you with a car. God will supply you with everything that you need. He's not almighty for nothing. I'm talking about a God who is willing to supply the best for His children. His love is everlasting.

God controls the time. He decides when He wants to bless you. All you have to do is be patient. It's that simple. God is not asking you to do much, but you have to be willing to do something for God. Don't be selfish; trust in God.

My brothers and sisters, you should be praising God for the marvelous works that He displays. Don't limit yourself when it comes to blessing God. Be glad to serve the Lord. Always keep God on your mind. Most importantly, remember that He's in control.

HONOR HIM

The Lord is a God of many great wonders. He is a revealer of dreams (Daniel 2:26-45). God is that force that understands what goes on in your mind and heart. He is a majestic God, therefore, you should honor Him.

Thou art worthy, O Lord, to receive glory and honor and power: for thou hast created all things, and for thy pleasure they are and were created (Revelation 4:11). God created man in His own image (Genesis 1:27). When He created us, He didn't make any mistakes. We should all give thanks to God for doing a marvelous job. He is a righteous King.

O come, let us worship and bow down: let us kneel before the Lord our maker (Psalm 95:6). God is worthy to be praised. We should not take Him for granted. Although we may sin, He is always there to forgive us. No matter what we do, God will always love us.

God is a Spirit: and they that worship him must worship him in spirit and in truth (John 4:24). The only way to worship God is in the Spirit because the Lord doesn't dwell in flesh. When you worship the Lord, you will gain strength. Worship God in truth because He doesn't deal with liars. All you have to do is be honest with God, and yourself.

We should all give thanks to God for being in our lives. He is good to everyone. The Lord loves everyone. He knows that we all make mistakes. My brothers and sisters, continue to honor the Lord because He is a holy King that always rewards His servants.

IN DUE TIME

Many of us want things fast. Some of us just don't have enough patience to wait. We say that we trust in God, but we can't wait on Him. My brothers and sisters, just relax because in due time, He will bless you.

God does not lie. He said He is going to bless you, and believe me, it shall come to pass. God has many blessings in store for you. It is up to you to be patient until He opens the storage room, and supply you with your blessings.

God has hope for all of us. Love God like He loves us. He never quits on His children, but some of us quit on Him. God is willing to bless us. We have to be willing to bless Him. Show God how much you love Him because He is going to show you how much He loves you. Trust me; in due time all of your desires are going to be fulfilled, so give thanks and glorification to the Almighty God.

JUST KNOW THIS

God is the key to success. Without Him, you can't make it. God will open doors for you that you thought could never be opened. Sometimes God may have you knocking down doors. That is why I love the ministers that God chooses. Again, understand me clearly. I love the ministers that God chooses. You know the ones that tell the truth. The ones that don't tell half-truths. The real deal ministers. And so, let me speak the truth to you. Understand this, my brothers and sisters; God is not a half God. He is a complete God, which means whole. And He wants you to be whole.

God just loves it when His children obey His every command. It fills Him with exuberant joy. The joy that He feels, He allows His children to feel. He also is not selfish. He provides His children with the same things that He has. What do you think, "in earth as it is in heaven" (Matthew 6:10) means? It means that God wants to provide the things that He has in heaven to you. In heaven, there is joy, peace, love, kindness, gentleness, caring, patience, and humbleness, just to name a few. Why should you not want those things? God wants you to have them.

Check this out my brothers and sisters. Whatever you are going through at this very moment, God already knows how He is going to bring you out. Don't wonder about it, and don't be double-minded about it. Just depend on God and you will see your way through. Be happy, for God is in control. The battle is already won, so that should tell you that God has your prosperous future in His hands. Count it all joy when you are in the wilderness because once you step into the land flowing with milk and honey you will say, "It was worth going through the wilderness." May God, Jesus Christ, and the Holy Spirit be with you. And just know this: the Holy Trinity loves you.

JUST PRAY

My brothers and sisters, we all go through hard times. It's how you face those hard times that make you a bold soldier or a weak one. Face the storm that comes upon you in your life. All you need to do is pray, and God will be there to help you. When you pray, you have to believe. You've got to have faith that the Lord will be there to help you. He is a trustworthy God on whom everyone can depend. Open your heart to Him. I promise you, He won't fail you.

And this is the confidence that we have in him, that, if we ask anything according to his will, he heareth us: And if we know that he hear us, whatsoever we ask, we know that we have the petitions that we desired of him (1John 5:14-15). Those who have confidence in the Lord know that He will be there for them. Your heart and mind must be without doubt. When you ask the Lord for something, it makes Him feel good. It lets Him know that you have faith in Him.

The Lord never breaks a promise. He never forgets His promise. God hears your every cry and believe me, He will be there to comfort you. *Blessed be God, even the Father of our Lord Jesus Christ, the Father of mercies, and the God of all comfort* (2 Corinthians 1:3). God is the One who is going to bless you. He is the One who is going to heal you from all of your pain. Believe in God and trust in Him. He will open the doors for you. My friends, just pray, and know that God is the holiest King in the universe.

LEAN ON GOD

God is a graceful Father. He gives us the strength that we need to make it through each day. He is a God that has high hopes for us. What makes it more wonderful is that He is going to help us along the way. That's why we all should lean on Him.

The more you lean on God the easier your life would be. He will handle all of your worries. God will strengthen your mind. He will speak for you. God doesn't want any of us to fail. He is going to uplift us the way that He wants us to be. Man doesn't uplift the children of God, He does.

I will deliver thee, and thou shalt glorify me (Psalm 50:15). When you lean on God, He will deliver you from all evil. There is nothing more powerful than God. While you are still worrying about the same thing, God has already fixed it. Please don't try to fix things yourselves because it will stay broken. Let God be your plumber, and fix your heart when it is leaking. God will replace your heart with a pure heart. He will cleanse you from all of your sins.

Don't call yourselves getting upset with God because it won't work. You didn't make God; He made you. God will take care of everything for you. Just be patient. Sometimes I may get impatient, but God is there to remind me to endure. Always keep God on your mind and heart because He keeps you in His mind. You are never alone. God is present even when you think He's not. Continue to walk in God because He is a great Father to lean on.

LEAVE IT IN GOD'S HANDS

How are you doing my brothers and sisters in Christ Jesus? Jesus is a delightful Shepherd. I just love the way that He leads us sheep. His Father, God, is the Master Shepherd who is leading all of us through. My brothers and sisters, I just want to tell you that whatever problem you are having, leave it in God's hands.

First of all, when you leave it in God's hands, everything will work out for you. God will never mishandle your problems. He will take care of your every need. God will take away your pain. The problem that you are facing, someone else is facing it as well. What makes you think that God can't handle your problem? There is no problem that is too big for Him. God is the problem solver.

Moreover, once you leave it in God's hands, it will take a lot of weight off of your shoulders. God wants you to leave everything to Him. He is the One who is going to make everything all right. God doesn't want you to worry about a thing.

My brothers and sisters, God loves you with a passion. Don't depend on anyone, but God. He is the One that is going to lead you to the place that you belong. Trust in God, depend on God, and love God so that He can do wonderful works for you, and through you. Just leave it in God's hands and trust me, He will never close them.

LEND A HELPING HAND

One thing I try not to be is selfish. God doesn't appreciate a selfish person. You have to be willing to do things for people, like God is willing to do things for you. Lending a helping hand should be one of the most important things on our mind because unselfishness is a quality that we Christians should possess. It shows that we have good character.

In fact, the Heavenly Father blesses those who help others because when you help someone out, it makes that person feel good. I love to see a smile on a person's face when I lend a helping hand to him or her. Be a cheerful giver, because the Almighty loves a cheerful giver. *Every man according as he purposeth in his heart, so let him give; not grudgingly, or of necessity: for God loveth a cheerful giver* (2 Corinthians 9:7).

Moreover, people know that you have kindness in your heart when you are willing to help them. You not only make yourself look good, but most importantly, you make God look good. He was the One that anointed you with a generous spirit, so don't forget about Him. God will do anything for His people, so He expects you to be the same way if it's for the right reason.

Furthermore, help your neighbors because someday, you may need them to help you. That's why it's not good to be selfish especially during a crisis in your life because you may need someone to help you. *He that despiseth his neighbor sinneth: but he that hath mercy on the poor, happy is he* (Proverbs 14:21). There is no man on this earth wealthier than God. If all rich people combined their money, jewels, and possessions, they still would not have greater riches than God, so if God can lend a helping hand they can too. For that matter, we all should! Most importantly, God doesn't belittle anyone He treats everyone the same, and you should be the same way, so be kind and lend a helping hand.

LISTEN TO GOD

Trust me, people; I know that sometimes you feel like giving up. I, too, get sick and tired of Satan trying to attack my mind. That's why you've got to have God on your side, because you can't fight Satan alone. Satan is a pest. And so whatever you do, my friends, always listen to God.

First of all, when you listen to God, He will guide you the right way. One thing God does not do is mislead people. God is the truth and the light. As you are walking in the valley of the shadow of death, God will shine His light upon you. He knows that you get weak. The minute you get weak, He whispers His Word in your ears, empowering you to become strong.

Moreover, never close your ears to God. As soon as you close your ears to God, Satan will attack. He attacks when you let your guard down. Satan is sneaky. That's why the Holy Word refers to him as a snake. You see, Satan fears God. He knows when God is in the midst. When God is present, Satan flees into another direction. He doesn't like it when you talk about God, and hates it when you listen to Him.

I lead in the way of righteousness, in the midst of the paths of judgment (Proverbs 8:20). When you are led by God, nothing can stop you from reaching your goals. God will knock down anything that dares to step in your way. He is leading you down the path of righteousness; just continue to follow Him. The minute you slip, that's when Satan slides in; but get back up and follow God. The Almighty God is a perfect teacher who teaches great things; listen to Him, so you won't go wrong.

LISTEN TO THIS

My brothers and sisters, listen to this. The Almighty God is a tremendous God. On Him, we can depend. God poured His breath into our nostrils so that we can live. It's time that we recognize God, and count the blessings that He has poured down upon us.

Great is our God above all gods (2 Chronicles 2:5). There is no god like our Almighty God He is the One who created all things. He is the One who nature obeys. If only we would obey God like nature does the world would be a much happier place. But many times, we choose to be disobedient. Hearken unto the Lord's voice, obey His voice, and respect His voice. Trust me, God won't lead you astray. I have been serving God my entire life, and He has never forsaken me. It is we who forsake Him.

When did you ever hear that God is good just to a couple of people? *The Lord is good to all: and his tender mercies are over all his works* (Psalm 145:9). The Lord loves all of us equally. He doesn't treat any one person better than the next. He does have amazing grace for all of us. He gives us plenty of chances to do the right things in life. God never gives up on His children. He has confidence in us. That's why I'm going to continue to serve God, because it makes me feel good to have someone that is always beside me.

I'm glad that you are taking heed, listening to this. I hope this passage influences you to continue to worship and praise God. He is the One whom gives all of us mercy. Fellowship with others, and tell them how God has been wonderful to you. As you do that, watch how your Heavenly Father blesses you more and more because you recognize Him.

LIVE IN HONESTY

I love God because He is fair to everyone. God doesn't belittle anyone. God is always there even when you think He's not. He wants you to recognize Him. He also wants you to live in honesty.

God created man in His own image (Genesis 1:27), which means that He wants us to live the right way. He wants us to seek after His righteousness (Matthew 6:33). The right way to live is to stay truthful. As long as you are honest, you are not going to dig yourself into deep holes. Fibbing doesn't do anything but cause trouble. Many relationships fail because couples often lie to each other. But couples who experience successful marriages do so because of communication and honesty.

When you are truthful, God will bless you. He does not deal with liars (Proverbs 6:17&19). God wants you to be honest with people just like you are honest with Him. He knows whether you are telling a lie or telling the truth. God knows everything that goes on in the world. Anyone, who thinks that he or she can fool God, is fooling him or herself. If man can catch you in a lie, what do you think God can do? To be truthful, my brothers and sisters, living in honesty will take you a long way in life.

MEDITATE ON GOD

Be silent for a moment, and listen to your spirit. What kind of spirit do you have? What kind of spirit controls your mind? Think about that. If Satan controls your spirit, I know a way you can make him stop. Get to know God, and allow Him to take control of your spirit. Please just meditate on God.

When you meditate, it is important that you clear your mind of negative thoughts. Keep your mind on God, and God only. Tell God how much you love Him. He will show you guidance. He will give you peace. At all times, think positively; even when you are going through hell. If God brought Jesus out of hell, He can do the same for you.

While you are meditating, ask God for strength, and He will give it to you. God knows what your heart desires. He loves you with a passion. Let God use you as a vessel to help pull more souls in. Don't be selfish. Help someone get to know God. Keep in mind that someone helped you.

My brothers and sisters, God will bless you with a calm mind, and a calm spirit. God will enlighten you with joy. He will make you be a light for other people. Trust in God and know that He won't mislead you. God loves you too much to do that. If your mind is troubled, He will give you peace, and that's why I encourage you to meditate on God.

MY MOTHER

I thank God for sending me down to His wonderful earth. I'm glad that God blessed me with the mother that I have. She is not only special to me, but also to others. My mother means the whole world to me. She is strong, a positive role model, and a kind person.

First of all, my mom is a strong person. She has strong faith in God. My mother never lets anything or anyone get her down. When I need someone to talk to, she is always there to comfort me. She is like a strong vessel inside of me. When she is doing fine, I'm doing fine. My mother encourages me have hope and confidence in myself.

Moreover, Mama is a positive role model. She never does anything negative. With the help of God, Jesus Christ, and the Holy Spirit, she leads a nation down the right pathway. Family, friends, church members, and others come to my mom for guidance. My mother is always filled with joy. Whenever you are around her, you feel her peace and happiness. My mom is just fun to be around.

Furthermore, my mother is a kind person. She is always there to help other people. Every Sunday, she cooks a big meal for everyone. She is the epitome of *Soul Food*. Mama will help anyone in times of need or distress. She will be there to talk about God or life, in particular. With an open invitation, she welcomes people into our home and church. My mother is just a loving person.

It is so tremendous having the mother I have. A mother who is always there to comfort and give a kind word. My mom is the best in the world. She is the greatest gift that the Almighty God has granted to me. My mother is the leader of my family and Holiness, Spiritual, and Truth Church. She is not only strong, but also a positive role model and a kind woman of God.

NEVER LOSE SIGHT

Good morning, my friends. It's nice to see another day. This is a wonderful day that the Almighty God has created. He is a great God. This world that He created is beautiful. Don't take God for granted, and never lose sight of Him.

There is a way that seemeth right unto a man; but the end thereof are the ways of death (Proverbs 16:25). When you try to do things on your own, it won't work. No one on this earth is greater than Jesus Christ, our Lord and Savior. Jesus Christ had help from God. What makes you better than Jesus that you don't need help from God? I ask God for help everyday because I know I can't make it alone. If you know anyone that made it without the help of God, introduce me to him. If you know anyone greater than God, introduce me to him.

He that handleth a matter wisely shall find good: and whoso trusteth in the Lord, happy is he (Proverbs 16:20). Happy is he or she because they kept their sight on God. When you keep your sight on God, He will reward you with blessings. When you keep your sight on God, He will reward you with joy. When you keep your sight on God, He will reward you with peace. God never breaks a promise. God gives all of us grace, and He is the Lord of forgiveness.

A wicked doer giveth heed to false lips; and a liar giveth ear to a naughty tongue (Proverbs 17:4). Children of God, please separate yourselves from people like that. God knows you are willing to help them, but how can you help them when they are not willing to help themselves? I admonish you; don't hang around them because you may pick up their ways. If that happens, you will lose sight of God, which will cause you to fall into the same pit with those wicked doers. You will also find yourself slipping off the pathway. Keep your sights on God, and bless His holy name.

OPEN UP YOUR HEART

It's not easy being a servant of the Lord. That's why I thank Him for giving me strength. I thank Him for blessing me to have peace in my heart. Having peace in my heart gives me the opportunity to open up my heart to others.

First of all, when you open up your heart to others, you show them how much love you have for them. Many people in this world need love. They are not getting love from their homes, or anywhere else. Always offer your love to someone because they would appreciate it. Don't turn anyone down. Have you ever seen anyone seek love from the Almighty God and be turned down? No you haven't. God loves everyone. He doesn't have hate in His heart.

Moreover, love people in the same manner that God loves you. Sometimes it may be hard to show love to some people. In a situation like that, you pray for those certain individuals and leave it up to God. God is the problem solver, and He will do anything to lift up those individuals.

My dearly beloved friends, you should never give up on an individual. Don't forget that you used to be weak. Someone was there to open up his or her heart to you. We all need love. We all have to love each other like our Heavenly Father loves us. God doesn't put hate in our heart, He puts love in it, so be like God and open up your heart.

PERSONAL SAVIOR

We all wonder about things. We wonder about how we get up in the morning. I know who wakes me up in the morning; it is the Almighty God. You know, God is a good God. It is good to know that you have someone that you can depend on. God is that Someone I can depend on. He never turns His back on me. At times, I may be down, but God will be there to encourage me.

God loves all of us. If He did not love us, He would not have sent His only begotten Son to save us from our sins (John 3:16). It's time that we praise God to the fullest. It's time that we stop being selfish, and let God use us the way that He wants us to be used. We are all special to God, and there is a purpose why each of us is on earth. God gave each of us a job to do, and that job is to help Him and each other pull souls into the knowledge of His truth. That's why we go through trials and tribulations. God is testing our faith and love for Him. *And not only so, but we glory in tribulations also: knowing that tribulation worketh patience; and patience, experience; and experience, hope* (Romans 5:3-4).

My brothers and sisters, remembering to pray it is vitally important. When you pray, you get closer to God. Be consistent with your prayers, which means pray everyday. Don't talk to God in weakness, but in boldness. *Let us therefore come boldly unto the throne of grace, that we may obtain mercy, and find grace to help in time of need* (Hebrews 4:16). As a witness, I can tell you what I experience in my everyday life. I pray daily, and as I pray, I get closer to God. So, stay encouraged in the Lord, and know that He is your personal Savior who will be there to help you in time of need.

PROBLEM SOLVER

Who is the problem solver? The Almighty God is the problem solver. He handles all my problems. He brings me out of all my troubles. God blesses me with everything I need.

Many are the afflictions of the righteous: but the Lord delivereth him out of them all (Psalm 34:19). The Lord delivers all of His children out of afflictions. Satan has many devices that he throws at the children of God. That's why we all have to stand tall in the Lord because we can't overcome evil without His help. Whoever says that he or she can defeat Satan without Jesus Christ, is a liar. Satan would just look at you and laugh.

We all have to be prepared for the days of battle. It's not easy being a servant of the Lord. It takes a lot of hard work and prayer. When you pray, ask the Lord for strength. As a Christian living in a world of sin, you are going to need it. We all have problems, but the Lord will take care of them because He is the problem solver.

PROVIDER OF JOY

I would rather be happy than to be sad. I'd rather be happy than to be mad. Living in this world, God knows there are going to be times that we are going to be mad, and sad. Let God who is the provider of joy, free you from anger and gloominess.

My soul shall be satisfied as with marrow and fatness; and my mouth shall praise thee with joyful lips (Psalm 63:5). When the Almighty God provides you with joy, you will become slow to anger. With the joy that the Almighty God is going to provide you with, there won't be any time for you to get mad. Your problems will become overshadowed by the joy that the Almighty God is going to provide you with. Instead of you worrying about your situations, you will be rejoicing in His holy name.

For our heart shall rejoice in him, because we have trusted in his holy name (Psalm 33:21). All you have to do is invite Jesus Christ into your heart. When you invite the Lord into your heart, He will handle everything for you. The Lord will bless you with a calm spirit. He will take away all of your worries. The joy that the Lord is going to provide you with is exceedingly powerful. His joy is so powerful that He can make King Kong shout His name with gladness.

They that sow in tears shall reap in joy (Psalm 126:5). There will be no more sad tears once the Lord blesses you with joy. He will completely fill you with happiness. Many will wonder why you smile and laugh all the time. Some may even think you are crazy, and always up to something. Those who understand jubilation will know that it is because you've been joymatized by the provider of joy which is the Almighty God.

SERVE GOD AND DON'T GET MAD

My Christian saints and friends, let's get real. Why do we get mad? I'm here to tell you, don't get mad. We should all be glad for we serve the Almighty God. It feels good to serve God, knowing that He's not a boss that will reward you unfairly. He will not keep your salary from you. Just as your boss on your secular job rewards you with a paycheck, God rewards you with blessings. But if you don't work, you don't get paid. Just like man rewards you according to how you work, God does the same based on how you serve Him.

God is the One who tells you to obey your masters (or bosses) on this earth (Ephesians 6:5-8). If you serve God a little, then your reward will be little. If you bless God a little, then you'll get blessed a little, so don't get mad. It makes no sense to get angry at those who have nice houses, cars, a wonderful spirit, and favor from God. I'm not saying that you don't have a wonderful spirit. I'm trying to get you to understand where the Holy Spirit is coming from. He's speaking through me to tell you not to get mad. You can have the same things and even more. All you have to do is increase yoru servitude to God. Give Him big blessings. Give Him more of your time. That's how you get favor. That's how you get God to pour blessings down upon you.

God is waiting for you to do more for Him. He is an eternal God. All you have to do is make the effort to do what you have to do for Him and do it. A big key to getting favor from God is blessing others. I'm not talking about with material things or worldly possessions, but with spiritual blessings such as motivating, encouraging, inspiring, reading the Word to them and pouring positive things into their spirits. Those who do that are the ones that you hear about. It's not too late for you to handle your business for God; and remember, it's not all about you, it's all about God. Don't forget who put you on top of the ladder. God is the key to His servants' success so, *serve the Lord with gladness: come before his presence with singing* (Psalm 100:2).

SMOOTH OPERATOR

The Lord is a marvelous God. He does everything in a perfect way. God makes sure that His animals are fed, and His plants are watered. He does a great job taking care of nature. The Lord is a smooth operator.

First of all, God does a great job motivating His children. He makes certain that their hearts are filled with confidence. God just wants His children to have faith, *the substance of things hoped for, the evidence of things not seen* (Hebrews 11:1). The Lord wants us to see things in the spiritual realm. If you are of the Lord, you don't live in the flesh, but in the spirit. *For ye are all the children of God by faith in Christ Jesus* (Galatians 3:26).

Moreover, God blesses His children with patience. To get any gift, or reward from God, you have to have patience. Don't be in such a hurry to get things because God will supply you with everything you need *that ye be not slothful, but followers of them who through faith and patience inherit the promises* (Hebrews 6:12). The Lord wants you to have faith, and believe that He will bless you *for ye have need of patience, that, after ye have done the will of God, ye might receive the promise* (Hebrews 10:36).

The Lord loves all of His children. He blesses us in a special way. Everything that He created is unique. God is that dream that we hope to see come true. My friends, God is just a smooth operator.

STAND TALL

God is a merciful Lord. He is a great Father to all of His children. His blessings are poured down on us like rain. Whenever we make the right decisions in life, God rejoices. There's nothing that we can do to make God stop loving us. His love lasts eternally. Therefore, God wants us to stand tall.

Even though you are living in the world, don't live of the world. God knows it's not easy because of the sinful nature that the world contains. In the midst of our temptations, He wants us to hold on to Him. There are many things in the world that tempt us to do ungodly things, but don't give in to it. Just remember that God is always with you.

My beloved sisters and brothers, I love you. As your brother, I'm going to continue to talk to you through my writings. Love God with all of your heart. Finish the work of Jesus Christ with your whole heart. Jesus Christ died for all of your sins. He was the ultimate sacrifice. Since Jesus Christ took such punishment for us, we could at least stand tall against the principalities of Satan, who is the ruler of sin.

STAY POSITIVE

Whatever you do, my brothers and sisters, stay positive. There is nothing that can stop you from reaching your goals. *I can do all things through Christ which strengtheneth me* (Philippians 4:13). Always keep that in your hearts. Know that the Lord is on your side. Know that the Lord won't forsake you.

Staying positive gives you confidence. In your heart, you feel that you can do anything. The God that you serve is positive, so you should be the same way. Don't be associated with those that are negative because the only thing they would do is bring you down. When you are positive, you will draw attention. People will love to be around you. With your positive spirit, you make people feel good. Your affirmative outlook helps them feel optimistic.

The more people come around you, the better that they will feel. It's just like when you are around the Almighty God. He makes you feel great. He shows you love. God doesn't make anyone feel bad for He loves all of us. God wants all of us to be a light, so stay positive, and let your light shine throughout the world.

THE GREATEST BOOK TO BE IN

We always hear people talk about how they would love to be in the Hall of Fame or in a magazine or newspaper article. I'm not saying that those things are bad because I would like to be in them as well. But I just would like to tell you, in the name of Jesus Christ, that the greatest book to be in is the Book of Life (Revelation 20:12). The Book of Life is the most famous book in the universe besides the Holy Bible. The Book of Life contains the names of those who are going to inherit the kingdom of heaven. The Book of Life contains the names of those who are joint heirs with Christ. While they were living on earth, the people listed in this book showed love to God and Jesus Christ. They are the ones who truly allowed the Holy Spirit to guide them.

The Book of Life, in which I believe the names are written in red, representing the blood of Jesus Christ, is written by Almighty God. Jesus Christ is waiting to see the ones whose names are written in The Book of Life. He is just waiting to have fun with them for all eternity. God is telling Jesus to be patient for the time is going to come for Him to see them.

My brothers and sisters, I believe that your name is written in The Book of Life. Be happy that your name is among those listed. Your name is in there with Abraham, Moses, Sarah, Paul, David, Daniel, the Hebrew Boys, Noah, and the rest of the great people of God in the Bible. Start praising God for the Book of Life.

Thank Jesus Christ for dying for your sins, and for God raising Him from the dead. If it weren't for Jesus Christ coming to earth, and dying for your sins, you would have no place in heaven or the Book of Life. The name of the book is The Lamb's Book of Life. The Lamb represents Jesus Christ, so don't wait until God opens the gates of heaven to rejoice. Begin rejoicing now; for you already know that you are in The Lamb's Book of Life, the greatest book of all.

THE HOLY KING

There is a King who is the ruler of everything. This King sits high, and looks low. He also makes perfect decisions. The King to who I'm referring is the Almighty God. Heaven is His throne; the place where He looks upon all of His children. He is a Shepherd that watches over His sheep, which are His children. He won't allow anyone or anything to harm them.

The Almighty God is the Holy King. He treats His servants with great love and respect. He also gives everyone an equal opportunity to seek Him. The great thing about the Holy King is that He will help you along the way. *In all thy ways acknowledge him, and he shall direct thy paths* (Proverbs 3:6). The King of peace will guide you through life's troubles. He will instruct you to make the right decisions in life. When you make a mistake, He will be there to correct it.

For this God is our God forever and ever: he will be our guide even unto death (Psalm 48:14). The Lord will direct you to the path of righteousness. His way is the key to eternal life. God will be your navigator along the pathway. With the light of His salvation, He will brighten the path for you.

There is no other king like the Almighty God. He is a King who welcomes everyone to His throne. The Lord wants everyone to celebrate with Him. Hope that the Lord chooses you to be a part of the celebration, because He is the Holy King.

THE HOLY ONE

Who is the Holy One? The Almighty God is the Holy One. Through a virgin, He sent His only begotten Son to save us from all of our sins. *And the angel answered and said unto her, The Holy Ghost shall come upon thee, and the power of the Highest shall overshadow thee: therefore also that holy thing which shall be born of thee shall be called the Son of God* (Luke 1:35).

God is in the midst of the church, so we should not be ashamed to praise Him. *Wherefore God is not ashamed to be called their God: for he hath prepared for them a city* (Hebrews 11:16). Just like He did with Abraham, Sarah, Abel, Noah, Joseph, Moses, Enoch, and Isaac, God will prepare a city for us, and He will not be ashamed of us if we have faith in Him.

Jesus Christ rebuked Satan, and told him that His Father is already rich. When a storm passes through, the Almighty God keeps our house standing. When we are hungry, He feeds us. When we are thirsty, He gives us something to quench our thirst, but like the Israelites, we still want to tempt God.

Never be afraid of what Satan can do because the Holy One is on your side. He will be there to shield and protect you. Some of us just don't know that the Holy One has already prepared a place for us. All we have to do is seek Him. God is a rewarder of them that diligently seek Him (Hebrews 11:6). *Be silent, O all flesh, before the Lord: for he is raised up out of his holy habitation* (Zechariah 2:13).

THE PROMISE KEEPER

Smile, for God loves you. Rejoice, for He created you. One thing God doesn't do is lie. Sometimes you may feel that things are not going to happen for you. I'm here to tell you not to worry because things are going to happen for you. Whatever God says He is going to do for you, He is going to do it; because He is the Promise Keeper.

First of all, you have to believe in God. Believe that God will make a way for you. Believe in God with passion. God just wants the best for His children. Sometimes you may feel that God is too slow. God is not a slow moving God. He just wants you to be patient. God is always on time, and His time is the best time. He knows the time better than everyone in this world.

Moreover, you have to hold on to God. Friends, times will get rough for you. When that happens, you have to keep your faith in God. Satan is going to do many things to tackle your mind, but you have to rebuke him. Keep pressing toward God with all your strength and heart. He will be there to help you throughout your life. Hold on to God because He has all the power to defeat Satan.

My beloved friends, get to know God each day as you live. He has been a wonderful Father to me. Trust in Him with your mind, heart, body, and soul. *Anything you ask, and it shall be given you; seek, and ye shall find; knock, and it shall be opened unto you: For everyone that asked receiveth; and he that seeketh findeth; and to him that knocketh it shall be opened* (Matthew 7:7-8). Now, by you believing in God, holding on to Him, and reading those two verses in Matthew, you should know that He is the Promise Keeper; a God who never breaks a promise.

THE TRUE SHOT CALLER

Check out the Almighty God! He is so fabulous by the way He works things out. God makes small blessings into big blessings, and large blessings into larger blessings. Trust me; God can do anything. God is the True Shot Caller. He calls the shots on everything. He tells the sun where to set. God tells the rain when and where to fall. He tells the natural disasters what places to skip over. I mean, God is amazing.

Everything He does is for good. Many people think that God does not exist. I'm here to tell you that He does exist. Who puts breath in your body so you can live? Who gave you legs so you can walk? Who gave you a mouth so you can talk? The Almighty God gave you those things. God created you and He can break you. He created you out of dust, and He will put you back in dust.

Continue to hold on to God because He will be happy to bless you. God has many blessings to give everyone if they would just believe in Him. God doesn't beg anyone to do anything. I love God, and I will do anything that He tells me to do. We all have to be that way. Once you open up your heart to God, and walk in His ways, watch how everything good happens for you. God is the True Shot Caller; the One who always calls the shots.

THE ULTIMATE JUDGE

It's great when you are serving someone like the Almighty God, the One who provides you with everything that you need. God has enough love for everyone. His love lasts eternally, which means forever. The Lord is not only our Master, but He is also the Ultimate Judge.

God looks at everything that each of us does. He takes records of the good things and records of the bad things that we do. He knows every thought and feeling that we have in our hearts. There is nothing that you can do behind closed doors without God knowing it. No one can hide from God. No one can keep secrets from Him. God is everywhere you go.

There shouldn't be any excuse for anyone not to make it to heaven. God's Word, which is the Bible, tells and shows us how we should live our life. The Bible is our guide to eternal life, but we have to be willing to obey God's commandments. His only begotten Son took the sacrifice for us, and the majority of us are still not grateful. All God wants us to be is a living sacrifice for Him.

It's funny, but sad, when people think that they have more power than God. He is different from these earthly judges. All those who enter into heaven are going to be the innocent ones. God gives everyone a chance to plead their case when He reveals their life to them. God's sentence is not a jail cell, but hell, which is worse than any prison on earth. So, *submit yourselves therefore to God* (James 4:7) because He is the Ultimate Judge who always makes the final decisions.

TRUST IN THE LORD

Many Christians today are double-minded. They can't make up their mind on whom to serve. Just because they are Christians doesn't mean that they serve God. Most of them sin more than they bless God. It's great to read the Bible, but we also have to live according to it. When I read the Bible, I live according to it because I trust in the Lord.

The Lord will make everything good for you if you would just trust Him. Many of us have faith one minute, and then the next minute, we are filled with doubt. How can the Lord bless you if your mind is wavering? He is just asking you to do two simple things: have faith, and trust in Him. *Blessed is that man that maketh the Lord his trust* (Psalm 40:4). The man who makes the Lord his trust doesn't worry because he relies on God. When you rely on God, He will handle all your problems. When you rely on God, watch how all your blessings start flowing. At a twinkling of an eye, is how fast God will bless you.

Whatever you do, have faith in God. *They that trust in the Lord shall be as mount Zion, which cannot be removed, but abideth for ever* (Psalm 125:1). When you have faith in the Lord, nothing can stand in your way. The Lord will be your rod and staff. *The Lord is good, a strong hold in the day of trouble; and he knoweth them that trust in him* (Nahum 1:7). For example, some of us may say, "That brother is getting blessed with everything he asks for." He is getting blessed with everything he asks for because he trusts in the Lord. God will do the same thing for you if you would just trust Him. God treats everyone fairly. *Trust in the Lord, and do good; so shalt thou dwell in the land, and verily thou shalt be fed. Delight thyself also in the Lord; and he shall give thee the desires of thine heart. Commit thy way unto the Lord; trust also in him; and he shall bring it to pass* (Psalm 37:3-5).

WAIT ON THE LORD

My brothers and sisters, God is not a selfish God. He is a cheerful supplier. He knows what He is doing; all He wants you to do is wait on Him. My brothers and sisters, the greatest things happen for you when you wait. Allow God to prepare you so you can have the things that you desire. Allow God to prepare you for your future. He knows what your future holds. God does not want you to have less; He wants you to have the best. That's why He has to prepare you so you can be ready for the best.

If you go out there in the world and try to do things on your own, you would screw things up. If you rush to get a husband or a wife, you will screw things up because you are not ready. Allow the Holy One to prepare you. Get close to Him so He can mature you. God does not want you to get hurt. That's why you've got to wait on Him.

To every thing there is a season, and a time to every purpose under the heaven (Ecclesiastes 3:1). When it is your season to get a wife or a husband, it will happen for you. I'm not talking about someone that will mistreat you, but someone that will treat you with love and kindness. God doesn't bless you with an abuser He blesses you with a companion. It is you that get impatient and go out and connect with the wrong person.

God has everything mapped out for you. He predestined everything. He knows your spouse, house, how much money you are going to possess, and your children. He ordained everything for you. All you have to do is follow in His footsteps and rely on Him. The Lord has everything ready for you, but you have to be ready to receive those things. You are not going to receive anything until God feels that you are ready. You have to be prepared to get a husband or a wife. You have to be prepared to get a car. You have to be prepared to receive riches and possession of land. God has to mature you for those things because if you are immature, you will squander everything. My brothers and sisters, it is important to wait on the Lord because if we try to do things in our own power, we will get it wrong every time. Please don't try to move ahead of God.

WHO DO YOU THINK YOU ARE?

One thing you don't do is take God for granted. He is not a toy to be played with. It is sad when people refuse to praise Him. They just don't know how many doors that God can open up for them. Rebellious people are selfish people. They have a God who is willing to do all He can to open up the doors to the kingdom of heaven, but they refuse to do the works that He asks them to do. He doesn't even ask for much. All He wants us to do is praise His name.

God loves all of us. He treats each of us the same, and gives everyone an equal opportunity to get closer to Him. Who does mankind think he is, to get upset with God when He doesn't come when we want Him to? We are not God's boss. God doesn't need us, we need Him. What if God were to be selfish and not allow any of us to come to heaven? What if He just let everyone die and go to hell?

Look at all those things that God does for us. He blesses us to wake up in the morning. He blesses us with food, shelter, and clothing on our backs, but just like the sons of Israel, we still complain. He blesses us with transportation, but we still don't want to glorify His name.

Each of us needs to wake up and recognize God. He shows all of us mercy, and we should be happy that we didn't live during the Old and New Testament days because God didn't play. There is power in God's name. Since Jesus Christ came here on earth, and died for our sins God has shown us mercy.

I'm not here to judge anyone because I don't have the authority. I'm not better than the person sitting next to me. The only thing I'm saying is that God wants to be loved just like we want to be loved. It shouldn't hurt us to praise His name. *Praise ye the Lord. Praise God in his sanctuary: praise him in the firmament of his power. Praise him for his mighty acts: praise him according to his excellent greatness* (Psalm 150:1-2). For He is God!

WILLING TO FOLLOW

Jesus Christ doesn't have any hate in His heart. The only thing He hates is evil. Jesus Christ is our source to getting closer to God. With Jesus as your source, you are going to pass the course to getting closer to God, but you have to be willing to follow Him.

First of all, God gives you a choice to either serve Him or Satan. He doesn't force you to do anything. If you serve God, you are going to live eternally. God is the provider of everlasting joy. He is the One whom you should worship daily. God is the epitome of holiness.

The Lord is with you, while ye be with him; and if ye seek him, he will be found of you; but if ye forsake him, he will forsake you (2 Chronicles 15:2). It's quite simple. The more you seek after God, the closer you are going to get to Him. Everywhere you go, God will be there. He will never forsake you. You are never alone as long as you keep God in your heart. God will be your shield in the days of battle.

The Lord is good unto them that wait for him, to the soul that seeketh him (Lamentations 3:25). God loves those who are patient. Those who are patient receive the greatest blessings. God wants all of your attention. Everyone should spend time with Him each day.

I love God because He's been so great to me. He never forsook me. I want everyone to serve God. He has enough blessings to supply everyone in this world. He loves each and every last one of us, so draw nigh to Him and be willing to follow.

WORK HARD

One thing I try my best to do is work hard. God loves the children that work hard. You not only have to work hard for God, but you have to work hard for the ones that He appoints over you. If you disobey your boss on earth, you are disobeying God, and that's not good. *Servants, be obedient to them that are your masters according to the flesh, with fear and trembling, in singleness of your heart, as unto Christ; Not with eye service, as men pleasers; but as the servants of Christ, doing the will of God from the heart* (Ephesians 6:5-6).

First of all, God blesses those who work hard. *The Lord shall open unto thee his good treasure, the heaven to give the rain unto thy land in his season, and to bless all the work of thine hand: and thou shalt lend unto many nations, and thou shalt not borrow* (Deuteronomy 28:12). God is not lazy, so you should not be lazy. Now, there is a difference between lazy and resting. To be lazy is to be unwilling to work; moving slowly; sluggish. To rest is to cease from all work, activity, or motion. God allows us to rest; even He rested when He finished His work. *And God blessed the seventh day, and sanctified it: because that in it he had rested from all his work which God created and made* (Genesis 2:3).

Consider this: what makes you better than God that you should not work? I had to realize that for myself because I know that I'm not greater than He. I have a long way to go to reach Him. Even His Son, Jesus Christ, worked. *Jesus saith unto them, My meat is to do the will of him that sent me, and to finish his work* (John 4:34). There should not be any excuse for anyone not to work hard for God. The only way to get to God is through Jesus Christ. If you don't get to Jesus, there is no way you are going to get to God. Whatever you may do, work hard and bless God, because He deserves all of your attention.

YOU ARE NEVER LONELY

What's going on, everybody? How are you doing? You know, today is a wonderful day to serve the Lord. Every day is good to serve the Lord for He blesses you to see the sun rise and set in each one of them. I just want to tell you that you are never lonely as long as you have God in your life.

I will not leave you comfortless: I will come to you (John 14:18). The Almighty God will be there with you every step of the way. When you are feeling low, He will be there to uplift you. God will put a smile on your face so bright that it will light up a whole room. The Almighty God is a Lord of comfort. He will be there to comfort you in your weakest hour.

The Lord will take heed to your cry. Because of the great Father that He is, He will be there to dry your tears. God will talk to you, and help you make it through your problems. He will not leave you in sorrow. The Lord is filled with everlasting joy. He will shower you with His love, kindness, and tender mercies.

My brothers and sisters all over the world, get right with God. Whatever ungodly thing you are doing, please stop. The idea of spending eternity in hell is not a pleasant thought. I know some of you do things that are displeasing to God so that you can have friends. Once you all Christ to head your life, you don't have to worry about making friends. God will bring people to you. Some days you may feel lonely, but always remember you are never alone, because God is there with you at all times.

Chapter Two

MOTIVATIONAL

A CLOSE RELATIONSHIP

The best thing to have is a close relationship with God. God understands all things. He understands why things happen. When you experience something bad, God will be there to encourage you. When you are feeling sad, He will bring you joy. God will never neglect you. If you have anything on your mind that's troubling you, take it to God and He will ease it. When you need encouragement, God will be there. When you need strength, He will be there. When you need love, He will be there. That's why I have a close relationship with Him.

God has everything that you need. He says you should not have a want for anything. He already knows what you need. Simply remain focused on Him. When you make God your focal point, you don't worry about anything, for you know He will take care of everything. God is a King who is always there to provide His servants with riches. If there is something that you don't understand, call on God, for He will help you, and that's why I say the best thing to have is a close relationship with Him.

A DAILY DELIGHTMENT

Good morning, my brothers and sisters. Today is a lovely day. Did you thank the Lord for blessing you to see it? God has given you another chance to glimpse His marvelous creation. The brightness of the sun is amazing. The heights of the trees are unique. The depths of the seas are astonishing. Who created these beautiful features? Your Heavenly Father the Almighty God.

Show God how much you appreciate His works. Give God the praise that He most absolutely deserves. He is perfect in everything that He does. He loves those who keep Him in their minds and hearts. Don't get me wrong; God loves everyone. His love is everlasting. Whatever you do, keep His commandments because keeping God's commandments lets Him know that you love Him. God just wants you to know that He is always by your side. My brothers and sisters, God is a daily delightment.

A GOOD APPEARANCE

My brothers and sisters, you know it's important to have a good appearance. Wherever you go, keep yourself looking good. Your Heavenly Father wants you to look good. My friends, you are representing God. Your desire to have a good appearance doesn't mean that you think you are all that. Turn a deaf ear to the negative things that people will say about your determination to look your best. There are going to be people who will say that you are stuck on yourself, but don't let that get you down, continue to look good. Show everyone the grace that God has given to you. You are not only good on the inside, but also good on the outside. Those who are jealous can't handle that. Jesus Christ was a handsome man. He had many people talking about Him, but He kept going and you must do the same.

Have some class about yourself. You may be from the ghetto, but that doesn't mean you have to act or look like it. God wants His children to have a good appearance. He trains His children to make a good impression. You can't go to a job interview, looking disheveled, and expect to get hired. You have to present your potential boss with the best you that you can possibly be.

My brothers and sisters, remember that a good appearance not only shows that you have respect for your Heavenly Father, but for yourself as well.

A GREAT GIVER

Everyday, I think about how great God has been to my family. He has brought us from a long way. God has poured down His blessings on all His children. He is truly a great giver. He has given us the ability to preach, and to teach. God is willing to share His blessings with all of us. He has so many blessings that they can cover the whole earth. God has anointed all of those who really desire to do His works. He takes care of His children. He blesses us with a nice place to stay and with cars that take us from place to place. The best things that I like that God has given to us are a pure mind, and a pure heart. With a pure mind, we keep ourselves thinking positive thoughts. We can continuously meditate on God. With a pure heart, we open ourselves to others. We are willing to love our neighbors, and share with them. The greatest gift I love that God has given to us is Jesus Christ, His only begotten Son. Jesus Christ made a way for us. He sacrificed Himself by dying for our sins.

Now, do you understand why I say that God is a great giver?

A LETHAL WEAPON

God is a powerful force. When it comes to His children, He shields and protects them. He doesn't like anyone bothering His little ones. His children are His sheep, which He pastures 24 hours each day. God is a lethal weapon. Remember what happened to those men who carried Shadrach, Meshach, and Abednego to the fiery furnace; they were burnt to death (Daniel 3:22). Instead of Daniel being eaten by the lions, the men who were responsible for him being thrown into the lions den were eaten along with their wives and children (Daniel 6:24). Remember how God destroyed the city of Sodom and Gomorrah (Genesis 19:24-25). There is no man, army, or beast on this planet that can stand up to God. There is no one who can defeat God. The fight won't last for a second.

Furthermore, there is no one who can hide from God or run from God. God can destroy everyone on this planet by simply snapping His fingers. He shows all of us mercy. With His kindness, He blessed us to be beautiful creatures. *For if God spared not the angels that sinned, but cast them down to hell, and delivered them into chains of darkness to be reserved unto judgment* (2 Peter 2:4). What does that tell you? God is a lethal weapon.

A LETTER TO GOD

Dear God,

    I'm just writing You a letter to let You know how much I appreciate You. I thank You for living in me. I thank You for the wonderful blessings that You pour down on the church and me. God, You know You are the best Master that anyone can have. You don't ask for much. Many people cry about not getting blessed, but those are the ones that don't deserve to get blessed. How could You bless them when they don't bless You? I know You ask Yourself that all the time. God, I don't take You for granted. I thank You for blessing the earth with sunny and rainy days. You are so amazing; the way You change morning to night and night into day. How do You do that? I'm doing my best to live the way that You want me to live. It's not easy, but I'm trying. Tell Your Son, Jesus Christ, I said hello, and thank You for saving me from all of my sins.

    Bless me to play a big role on earth just as Your other servants did in the Old and New Testaments. God, use me as a vessel, and work through me, so I can help those who need You. Bless those who are weak, and bless the poor because they need You the most. God, continue to bless me to be strong and bold in You. Sometimes I might try to handle my business without You, but I never get it done. I need You in my everyday life, so I ask that You continue to be everywhere I go, because I can't live without You. Thank You for choosing me to work for You, and I love You.

Your servant,
Demetrice M. Gates

A MARVELOUS GOD

I love the Lord. Jesus Christ is my friend. Everyday, He blesses me with gifts. He blessed me with the gift to write. God is my Heavenly Father. When I call on Him, He is always there to answer me. He is a marvelous God. God blesses the earth with trees to help us breathe. He blesses the earth with plants to make the air smell good. God blesses the earth with steel to help us build. The way that He feeds the earth is so unique. With His rain, He feeds creatures in the sea, nature, and the human race. Without God, this earth would not survive. That's why I'm glad that He holds it in His hands. With the sun, He keeps us warm. With the wind, He keeps us cool. Whenever a storm approaches, He shields us from the devastations of it. When we are walking into danger, He warns us. When we are stressed, He relieves us. Now, do you understand why I say He is a marvelous God?

A POWERFUL FORCE

God is a powerful force. He treads upon His enemies like a tornado sweeps through a city. Everything He does is perfect, which means He doesn't make any mistakes. When God controls your mind and heart, nothing can go wrong. You have to believe that He's with you everywhere you go. And if you're unsure, all you have to do is plead the blood of Jesus, and He will be right there. Let God be your light just as He was with the Israelites, as He led them out of the land of Egypt (Exodus 13:21). As you pursue God, He will light His pathway for you. The path is not going to be easy because Satan is going to try his best to block you from getting closer to God. That's why you have to have faith in God, and believe that He won't allow Satan to cause you to detour off the path. To all of my Christian friends, God is also powerful when He is silent.

A POWERFUL SHIELD

God is a powerful shield. He is a shield that protects His children 24 hours a day. God is always present to protect His children from danger. With His force field, He stops evil forces from entering His children. He won't let any evil force harm them. Any ungodly thing that approaches them will immediately get shocked. God shields His children daily. It is a huge mistake to mistreat His little ones. Those who interfere with the children of God will have to pay for it. If they think that they are going to get away with it, they'll soon find out that it doesn't work that way.

When a person messes with the children of God, they have to deal with Him; and believe me, it won't be a pretty sight. Sinners can't get mad if saints serve God. Not only did He create us, but He also created them. Who does the enemy think he is? I tell you this; if he continues to mess with the children of God, he will be destroyed because God is a powerful shield that never lets His guard down. *For our soul waiteth for the Lord He is our help and our shield* (Psalm 33:20).

A SHINING STAR

God is a just Father. God builds His children with strength. He knows when they are feeling low. God is a shining star. Every place He goes, He stands out. The enemy knows when He is present. When God is presenting the midst, the enemy scatters away. God is all about peace. He speaks peace, eats peace, drinks peace, and rests with peace. To sum it all up, He is peace. God is that streetlight that is on when you are walking at night. He is that second wind that gives you a push when you are working out. He loves to be acknowledged by His children. He loves to be appreciated. God shines on every scene. He shines in the darkest places on earth. Before you fall asleep, look out of your window and check out the shining star. That's the Almighty God.

A SPIRITUAL CONVERSATION

A spiritual conversation is a good conversation. It involves the children of God talking about their Heavenly Father and personal Savior. All that can be heard is positive speaking. There is nothing profane that comes out of the children of God's mouths as they talk about God and Jesus Christ. When you are having a spiritual conversation, your thoughts and words are pure. It pleases God when His children talk about Him. God looks down upon us and smile as we acknowledge Him. He knows that His children love Him for He searches their minds and hearts. God says to Jesus, "Listen to the way that My children talk about Us. It's a good thing that We created them."

When you are having a spiritual conversation, it expresses the way that you feel about God and His Son. The best thing I love about a spiritual conversation is that you don't hear curse words come out of people's mouths. The conversation is pure, not filthy. As you talk about God and His Son, you get that wonderful feeling inside of you. You feel that you are being anointed. God blesses those who appreciate Him. My brothers and sisters, continue to have a spiritual conversation, for it shows that you are blessing your Heavenly Father.

A STRONG TOWER

Check this out, my brothers and sisters. God is a strong tower. He stands tall with might and power. On Him, you can lean in your weakest hour. He's the Creator whose blessings pours and showers. One thing God won't do is give up on you. No matter what you do, God will always love you. He is an unselfish God. Anything you need, He will provide it for you. Any trouble you get into, He will bring you out. Any mistake you make, He will gladly correct. God is a merciful Father. He gives all of His children grace. God is a stone wall that no one can run through; not even Superman. He's a ship that can't be sunk. God is a tree that can't fall down. He will protect you from all of your enemies, and that's why our God is a strong tower.

A TRUE EXAMINER

Listen, everyone. I just want to tell all of you that God is a true examiner. He examines everyone's heart. He knows if your heart is clean or polluted. God knows whether or not you care about Him. He knows if you are doing things from the heart or doing things just to glorify yourself. *O Lord, thou hast searched me, and known me, thou knowest my down sitting and mine uprising, thou understandest my thought afar off* (Psalm139:1-2). The Lord knows your every thought. He knows what you think about. He examines your mind to see if your thoughts are pure. When it comes to making examinations, God is serious because He is not going to dwell inside of an unclean vessel. He has to examine you to see what He needs to work on. It is for your own good.

When you go to the clinic, the doctor gives you an examination to see what he needs to work on. God does the same thing when He examines your spirit, so don't get upset. He is only here to help. He has to make sure that you are doing fine. God doesn't want you to have a handicapped heart, mind, or spirit. God wants you to be well equipped. He wants you to be prepared, because when you go to war, He doesn't want you to be overtaken by the enemy. If you are not ready, God is not going to send you out. The enemy will slaughter you. Trust me; God always knows what He is doing. *Search me, O God, and know my heart: try me and know my thoughts: And see if there be any wicked way in me and lead me in the way everlasting* (Psalm 139:23-24).

A TRUE MINISTER

God is a true minister. He ministers to all. He is someone you can count on to lead you the right way. God is the right way. He will lead you to the path of eternal life. God is eternal life. God does not lie. He is not a hypocrite. He is a perfect and just God. He knows everything about life. God knows the struggles that you face. He knows the pain that you experience. God is here to help you. Listen to Him. He will not mislead you. Put all of your trust in Him. Serve God with your whole heart.

He is a minister of guidance. He works great with those who are patient, and those who are willing to follow Him. God tells you the whole truth, not half of it. He will counsel you with any problem that you have. He is a great guidance counselor. The best part about it is that He won't try to get money out of you. God is willing to help you get through any problem or situation that you are having. If you want to know anything, or have something on your mind, take it to God, for He is a true minister who can help you with everything.

A TRUE SOLDIER

Check this out, my brothers and sisters. It is very important that you know this. Many of us claim that we are soldiers, but are we true soldiers? A true soldier is one who is willing to serve God no matter what storm he or she goes through. A true soldier does not complain; he or she gets the job done. He or she follows the orders of God. A true soldier knows that God is the head in charge. A true soldier is not afraid to die for God. He or she is ready for war.

God is the missile that is going to destroy the evil military. He equips His troops for battle. He makes sure that they are armed and ready. God is the generator of toughness. He trains His troops to be tough. When He puts His soldiers out on the battlefield, they destroy every evil thing. God commands His troops to destroy them all. He does not want any evil left standing. He is a mighty God and He wants His soldiers to be mighty. My brothers and sisters, strive to be a true soldier because it is an honor being on the battlefield of the Commander in Chief of the holy army.

ALL THINGS ARE POSSIBLE

What's up my friends? What's going on? I just want to tell you that all things are possible. You serve the Almighty God. Through Him, you can do anything. Through Him, you can become successful. With God, you are successful. There is nothing too hard for God. Set your goals, and go after them. Don't limit yourself. Use every gift that the Almighty God instilled within you. Don't let your gift be in vain. Show the world how good God has been to you. Any obstacle that you face, count it all as joy for you know the Lord will help you through it. All you have to do is believe in Him, and His begotten Son, Jesus Christ. Prove to God how much you love Him. Show God that you are ready to make it to the next level, and remember that *with God all things are possible* (Mark 10:27).

ALWAYS BE ON GUARD

What's up, my friends! How are you doing? I'm doing great because I have a great Father. I'm here to remind you to always be on guard. As soon as you step out of your home, Satan is waiting for you. Just like God has His children, Satan has his as well. Satan is everywhere. He's at jobs, schools, churches, homes, and in high places. That's why we have to be ready for him. God has given us the tools to be prepared for Satan. It is up to us to use those tools. We all have to be strong in the Lord and the power of His might because that is the only way to triumph over Satan. Satan is not weak; he is powerful, but not more powerful than the Almighty God.

Don't forget that Satan was once in heaven. He knows how powerful God is. That's why he is trying his best to destroy the children of God. Satan doesn't love anyone. He doesn't love himself, nor does he love the people who worship him. All he does is use them to do his evil work. He preys over innocent people.

Friends, continue to read your Bible, because God's Word is power. The more you read the Bible, the stronger you become. It is your guide to getting closer to God. Satan is a snake, and that's why we always have to be on guard and prepared to snap that snake's head off.

AN ADORING FATHER

God is an adoring Father. He provides His children with anything they need. He provides them with love, peace, happiness, wisdom, knowledge, and understanding. He is a caring Father. Whenever His children weep, He dries their tears. He gives His children great advice. God raises His children in the way that they suppose to be raised. He knows that they are not perfect. He knows that they are going to make mistakes. God always forgives His children whenever they do something wrong.

God puts a roof over His children's heads. He provides them with transportation so they can handle their business. His children don't have to beg for anything. God already knows what their hearts desire. He is a true provider. God whispers pure words in His children's ears. He pours His comfort into their hearts. He quenches their every thirst for righteousness. I mean, God is truly amazing. He knows when His children are troubled for He watches their every move. He searches their minds and hearts just to see if everything is okay. He is a great Father that rewards His children for doing the right things in life. My brothers and sisters, God is an adoring Father who always cares for His children.

AN EVERLASTING LOVER

The Almighty God is an everlasting lover. You don't have to worry about Him cheating. Put all your trust in God. He will never break your heart. God will be with you every hour of the day. He will eat breakfast, lunch, and dinner with you. God is a husband or a wife that you can depend on. He will pay your bills, car notes, loans, and insurance for you. You won't have any problems looking for God because He will be right beside you. When you think that He's not there, just page Him and He will call you. Hit God on the spiritual cell phone, and if He doesn't answer right away, leave a message. God talks to millions of people. Trust me, He will return your call. He is a wonderful force that you can depend on. God will never be unfaithful. He loves you too much to do that, and that's why I say He is an everlasting lover.

AN UNSELFISH GOD

God is an unselfish God. Look at the way that He blesses His children. He blesses His children to be healthy. He blesses His children to become successful. God gives His children comfort. Look at the way He blesses animals. He gave animals ponds from which to drink water. He gave animals plants from which to eat. He gave animals strong outer coverings to endure changes in the weather. Look at the way that God blesses nature. He blesses nature with sun and rain, to help trees and flowers grow. He is a wonderful God. That's why I say earth can't survive without Him. We all need God. God is full of love, and compassion. He is merciful. He shows everyone and everything how great His love is. Just like God blesses us, we also have to bless Him. We have to bless God with praises. We have to bless God by paying our tithes and offering. The more you bless God, the more He is going to bless you; for He is an unselfish God.

BE CAREFUL

Let me give you all a warning, be careful of who you let get next to you. There are many people out there in the world that are deceiving others without regard of the consequences. They live to deceive others. They live to play games. They live to hurt others. I just don't want it to happen to you. That's why I'm telling you to be careful of who you let get next to you because it happened to me. I let someone get next to me and that person was the enemy. That person deceived me, used me, and hurt me, but God brought me healing.

My brothers and sisters, there are people out there waiting to do it to you. Be on guard. Ask God to give you discernment because there are people out there who are wolves in sheep clothing. I'm getting sick and tired of my sisters and brothers getting hurt by deceivers. Those deceivers just don't know whom they are dealing with. They are dealing with God's children and when it comes to His children, He doesn't play. I love you, my brothers and sisters. I don't want you to get hurt. Your heart is precious. Don't let any fool come into your life and hurt you.

What is a fool? My definition of a fool is a person who doesn't care about hurting others. But every fool should know that in spite of their hurtful nature, they have people in the world that care about. Even Jesus Christ cared for people who ultimately turned against Him. My brothers and sisters, if people turned against Jesus Christ, know they are going to turn against you. *The disciple is not above his master, nor the servant above his lord* (Matthew 10:24).

My brothers and sisters, know that you don't need anyone to tell you who you are. Know that you don't have to be with a man or a woman to validate yourself because you are already validated through Jesus Christ. Just be careful about who you choose to be your friends, for you never know: they can turn out to be your worst enemy.

BE COMMITTED

In order for us to be strong in God, we have to be committed to serving Him. *If they obey and serve him, they shall spend their days in prosperity, and their years in pleasures* (Job 36:11). The children of God have to be a strong army to go up against the principalities of Satan. When God calls us to do something, we should not hesitate to do it because He is not a slow moving God. *And we know that all things work together for good to them that love God, to them who are the called according to his purpose* (Romans 8:28). We have to be willing to do the works that the Almighty commands us to do. The Lord never does anything to harm us because He loves His children. The Lord never gives us more than we can handle. It's time that we have faith, and trust in God. The Lord will heal you when you are sick. He will also be your shield in the day of battle, so why not be committed to an awesome force like Him!

BE FIRED UP FOR GOD

Good morning, my brothers and sisters. What a joyous day that God Almighty has created! I mean, He is a joyful God. My brothers and sisters, I challenge you to be fired up for God. Fired up for God means being pumped up for Him. When you praise God, be fired up for Him. When you talk about God, be fired up for Him; for He is not a God of sadness, neither is He a God of hindrance. Therefore, you should be happy to be fired up.

When a prophet tells you that God is going to wonderfully bless you, you get fired up. Why can't you get fired up to bless God? I'm not trying to judge you, I'm trying to motivate and encourage you. The more you get fired up for God, the more He shines in you. Even when you are having problems, be fired up for God, for He is bigger than your problems. Your determination to be fired up for God in the midst of your adversity will even amaze your neighbor. Your neighbor will look at you and say, "Man, that sister or brother is fired up in the Lord." Don't let anybody stop you from being fired up for God. Continue to praise, bless, and be encouraged in Him. God will say to Jesus and the Holy Spirit, "It feels good living in this individual." From this point on, my brothers and sisters, make an effort to stop complaining about your problems and situations, and instead, come to the Lord fired up.

BE HAPPY

I know you may be feeling down because one of our loved ones passed away, and that is okay because grieving is not a sin. My purpose today is to tell you to be happy. I know what some of you are thinking: "You must be crazy! My friend, a family member recently passed away and you are telling us to be happy." You are absolutely correct; I am telling you to be happy. Be happy, for no longer will Brother Ralph suffer. Be happy, for no longer will he worry about the troubles of this world. He does not want you to be sad, nor angry, because he is in the presence of the Lord; and when you are in God's presence, there is no room for sadness or depression. Right now, he is in the presence of the Lord, praying that we keep living. He is in the presence of the Lord, praying that we do not mourn over him. He is in the presence of the Lord, experiencing peace and joy. So rejoice, celebrate life and be happy, for Brother Ralph has returned to the King of kings and Lord of lords.

In loving memory of my uncle, Brother Ralph Mims.

BE HAPPY FOR OTHERS

It feels so good to have God in your life. God is a happy God, and He wants you to be happy. My brothers and sisters, happiness cries out. Be happy, my brothers and sisters, even if you have to force the positive emotion upon yourself. Be happy when you get blessed and be happy for others when God blesses them. God not only wants to bless you in the name of Jesus, He wants to bless others. When He does, rejoice with them. Thank God for blessing others. Do they deserve to get blessed? Do you deserve to get blessed? Think about it. None of us DESERVE God's blessings, but He showers us with them on a daily basis anyway, because He is a good God and He loves us.

Your neighbor works hard just like you do. Be happy when God blesses others with a car and a house. Be happy when others move to the top of the ladder. They love God just like you do. In fact, your being happy for them makes them feel good. I remember when my childhood basketball teammate walked up to me and told me that he made it to the National Basketball Association League (NBA). I was thrilled for him. My happiness for him put a big smile on his face. And so, instead of being jealous of others, let's be happy for them. Not only is there power in rejoicing for others, but greater still, it shows that we are of Christ.

BE PROUD TO BE MEN AND WOMEN OF GOD

My brothers and sisters, I just want to encourage you to be proud to be men and women of God. It feels good to be this way. Now let me be clear, I'm not talking about proud as in being arrogant because God hates arrogance (Proverbs 6:17). I'm talking about proud as in being confident and happy. It was this type of pride that Jesus Christ expressed during His triumphant entry into Jerusalem. He was proud of who He was in the Lord. He presented Himself as a King because He is a King. And so, my brothers and sisters, recognize that you are not only men and women of God, but also kings and queens. We are men and women of honor. God does not want us walking around with our heads down. The world wants us to be in bondage, but we have to refuse to be bound and oppressed. We have a Higher Power helping us. We have a Higher Power guiding us. It is time for us to recognize who we are and the power that we have.

Our Father created this world. Our Father created this universe. We have the divine right to be proud. Therefore, greet each other with love. Honor each other with respect. Let the world know that God raises excellent people. You see, the children of the world walk with their heads up high. Why can't we walk with our heads up high? So be it if they call us arrogant. So be it if they say we think that we are all that. They are right; we *are* all that! For God created us and brought us up right. Our God is worth more than houses, cars, and money. Our sovereign God has the richest throne in the universe. It excites Him when, inspired by His love, we decide to walk as He walked; that is, in authority with pride and distinction. And so, my brothers and sisters, be proud to be men and women of God, for your Father in heaven, your Creator, takes pride in having created you.

BE SLOW TO ANGER

Good morning, my friends. I'm glad that the Almighty God has blessed you to see another day. He does everything in an amazing way. This lets you know that you are special to Him.

The reminder that I offer to you today is to be slow to anger. What do you gain by being angry? Satan wants you to get angry. He knows that if he can upset you, you are more vulnerable to sin. That's why the Almighty God says, *be ye angry and sin not: let not the sun go down upon your wrath, neither give place to the devil* (Ephesians 4:26-27). God knows that sometimes you are going to get mad. Being angry is not a sin, but He wants you to be careful so your anger doesn't cause you to sin. Many people out there in the world dwell in rage. They let the spirit of anger control them, but you don't have to be like them. In fact, they are the ones who provoke you and others to get angry. Let God control your spirit. Always remember that *a soft answer turneth away wrath: but grievous words stir up anger* (Proverbs 15:1). My beloved brothers and sisters, don't cause anyone to get angry. If anyone tries to get you upset, just be polite to him or her. It let's your Heavenly Father know that you are slow to anger.

CALL ON GOD

God is the most wonderful force in the universe. His perfection surpasses everyone else's. His love runs deeper than anyone else's. God is that friend you need to call on when trouble arises. His phone line is never busy. You can talk to God about anything. He will feel your pain. God knows everything about you. He knows what you are facing in life. God will help you make it through anything. His power is unique beyond imagination. Take a look at the clouds; they are wonderful. Take a look at the stars; they are tremendous. Now, if God can create something as matchless as that, what makes you think that He can't help you make it through life challenges?

Take time to meditate on God. Open up your mind and heart our Father in heaven. Please don't let your mind waver because *the just shall live by faith* (Romans1:17). *Without faith it is impossible to please God* (Hebrews 11:6). Trust me, because I know sometimes it's hard to have faith; especially when you keep failing to achieve a particular victory. But hold on to God because He won't leave you hanging. You have to allow yourself to be a puppet in the hands of God. When you are a puppet in His hands, He controls your life. When you are a puppet for Satan, the strings get tangled. My friends, whatever the situation, just call on God. He will answer your every prayer.

CENTER OF MY ATTENTION

Who or what is the center of your attention? Well, God is the center of my attention. I make sure that I stay focused on Him. He is the reason for my existence, and knowing that He's the reason for my existence gives me reason to express my thankfulness and appreciation to Him for creating me. He sent His beloved Son, Jesus Christ, down here on earth to die for my sins. Then Jesus chose me as one of His sheep. He put me in two remarkable families, the Body of Christ and my earthly family. Last, but not least, He prepared a place for me. Therefore, God is the center of my attention because He is a tremendous God. He is a loving and peaceful God. He is a God of creativity. He is a wonderful artist and craftsman. He created you and me into wonderful beings. Look in the mirror and see for yourself, and perhaps, you will understand why God is the center of my attention.

CONTINUE TO DO GOOD

The children of God have a marvelous Father. They don't have to worry about anything. All they have to do is continue to do good. The Almighty God is good so He expects His children to be just like Him. God doesn't train His children to be bad. He is the greatest role model in the universe. He controls everything. The children of God are required to keep His commandments. Whenever He tells us to do something, He expects us to do it. He is our Heavenly Father, so we have to respect Him.

When we do good, it shows our Father that we obey Him. You can't be a knucklehead and expect to reap the promises of His blessings. You should want to do good, for God is always watching. Impress God by helping others. Show Him that you are concerned about your fellow man.

Some people are egotistical, only mindful about themselves. They give no consideration for what happens to those around them. How can anyone expect to get into the kingdom of heaven if they are selfish? God deals with people who care. He nourishes those who care. *Wherefore, let them that suffer according to the will of God commit the keeping of their souls to him in well doing, as unto a faithful Creator* (1 Peter 4:19).

DO WHAT YOU HAVE TO DO FOR GOD

My brothers and sisters, I challenge you to do what you have to do for God. Don't worry about what God is going to do for you because He always does His part. Whatever you do for God, do it with faithfulness. If you preach, sing, write, play an instrument, or dance, remain faithful in your servitude. God is faithful to you, so be faithful to Him. Whatever you do for God, do it with gladness (Colossians 3:23). Don't grudgingly do it, but do it in love. God doesn't hate what He does for you, and He does them without regrets.

The God that we serve is awesome. He would do anything to please His children. Doing what you have to do for God is a great thing. It's a great thing because you are working for the greatest boss in the world. When this boss rewards you, it is huge. But keep in mind, my brothers and sisters, you are not to don't do what you have to do for God just to receive His rewards, but do it because you love Him. He is a God with high hopes for you. He is a God with many great wonders. God will not hassle or hinder you. He will encourage you. Honor Him by doing what you have to do for Him.

DON'T BE ASHAMED

We say we serve a wonderful God, but if we truly believe that, why are we ashamed of Him? Why don't we spread the word of His goodness? It wouldn't hurt us to tell other people about the Lord. We can talk about everything else, but when it comes to God, we often stay silent. He is the world's greatest Father, and He deserves to be talked about. I have never had a boring conversation about God. I have fun when I share His message to others. God gives us joy. He is an interesting God.

The world is filled with fake people and artificial Christians. I'm just telling the truth. One minute, a so-called Christian is for God, and the next minute, he or she is mad at Him. It's time for us to make up our minds on who we want to serve. Time is running out. We are living in the last days. Jesus said, *For whosoever shall be ashamed of me and my words, of him shall the Son of man be ashamed, when he shall come in his own glory, and in his Father's, and of the holy Angels* (Luke 9:26).

Talk about your Heavenly Father. Tell others how He has been a blessing to you. The more you talk about God, the more blessings He is going to send down. You should be happy to talk about the Lord for He is a great Master to serve. God's children have no reason to be ashamed.

DON'T BE JEALOUS

Feel me on this. The same Spirit created us all, which is the Almighty God. Why do some of us want to be jealous? The person that we may be resentful of is no better than we are. We never know. That person whom we are jealous of can give us great advice. He or she can be a great blessing to us, but we miss the blessing by choosing to be envious. Instead of being jealous of one another, why can't we use our gifts that God has given us and help each other?

Be positive toward one another, and not negative. God created us to love each other, not to be jealous of each other. Don't get me wrong. Sometimes, I fall prey to jealousy, but through God's power, I get over my egotistical ways. God knows that we are not perfect, but we should help each other reach that point – that is, perfection, wholeness, or completeness in God. It's okay that you don't have good looks like the next person. It's okay that you don't have a house or car more expensive than the next person. God still loves you. He loves all of us the same. My brothers and sisters, just continue to work hard and don't be jealous.

DON'T BE SELFISH

My brothers and sisters, whatever you do, don't be selfish in your dealings with God. He is the One who wakes you up everyday. He is the One who protects you from all of your enemies. He is the One who showers blessings down upon you. Promise God that you won't be selfish to Him, and please Him by serving Him, and by being a blessing to others. Look at the beautiful children that God blessed you to have. Look at the nice home that God blessed you with. Look at your family members that God delivered and saved. My brothers and sisters, I'm talking about a God who loves you no matter what you do. His love is extraordinary.

My brothers and sisters, just feel me on this. When you were all alone, who was there for you? When you were sick, who was there for you? When you were hurt, who was there for you? It is the love of God. Give God thanks and appreciation. Praise God with joyfulness. Let God know how much you admire Him. It hurts me when someone speaks against God, but what this person needs to understand is that God was the One that created her. That person needs to know that God is the One that truly loves him. Be compassionate toward God. Love, honor, and adore Him. He sent His Son to die for you. Selfish is not in His vocabulary for He is a generous God.

My brothers and sisters, let us all bow down before God to let Him know that we respect Him; and out of our love and respect for Him, we refuse to be selfish, but selfless.

DON'T FORGET ABOUT GOD

What's up, saints of God? What's going on? The best things start to happen for you when you put your trust in the Lord. I know that trusting in the Lord is the best decision you have made in your life, but I just have to remind you to not forget about God. All you have to do is keep God on your mind. Bless God by paying your tithes and offerings. Praise Him each day as you live. Tell more people about Him. Tell them how God made you into who you are today. Personally, I get so leery of people who forget about God. All their lives they cry and complain about not getting blessed, but once they get blessed, they forget about God. No doubt, God just sits in heaven and shakes His head. No one that exists or has existed on this planet is above God. There is no one who has more power or riches than He. Hence, it won't hurt you to open your Bible and read it. It won't hurt you to brag about God. God is the One who blesses you to be successful. And so, my brothers and sisters, no matter who you are, your status or accomplishments; please don't forget about God.

DON'T GIVE UP

Hello, everyone; it's me again. Rejoice for the Lord has blessed you to see another day. I'm always doing great because the Lord is everywhere I go. Whatever you do, have faith in God and don't give up. Life is a challenge, and only the strong survive. Each day, you face a new challenge. The children of God face challenges on a daily basis because Satan is out there waiting for us. Satan is is the ultimate evil-doer, and he would do whatever it takes to destroy the children of God. That's why we have to be equipped with the armor of God (Ephesians 6:11).

Now, there are going to be people who are going to be against you. Such adversity comes with the territory of being a child of God. Remember what happened to Jesus; He had stones thrown at Him (John 10:31-39). The Jews, some of His own people, rejected Him. You must continue to walk as children of the light. Show your Father that you do have faith in Him. When you do the right thing, you make Him proud. My friends, continue to walk boldly in the Lord, and don't give up because you are more than a conqueror (Romans 8:37).

DON'T MESS WITH GOD'S INVESTMENT

This is for the people who act like they don't know. God is a tough God. He isn't afraid of anyone. Fearless is an appropriate nickname for Him. He doesn't let anyone push Him around. To all of those who think that they are big and bad, try messing with God or His investment, and watch your results. It wouldn't be a pretty sight.

God's investment is His people. His people are bought with a price, which is through the shed blood of Jesus Christ, His remarkable Son, and right hand man. If you don't believe me, read Exodus 14:21-31. God took the Egyptians out for messing with His investment, the children of Israel.

For those who act unknowledgeable about the identity of God's investment, I'm going to make it plain and simple. It's that person who loves his or her neighbor. It's those who preach and teach the Holy Word of God. Just to break it down a little further, His investment is those who worship God in spirit and in truth. Don't mess with them. Instead, make it a priority to become part of the investment. Turn away from wickedness and ask God for forgiveness. Follow after Jesus Christ and grow in grace. Love and adore Him, and tell your enemies, "Don't mess with me because I'm God's investment; an investment you don't want to tamper with."

DON'T PLAY WITH GOD

Let me give everyone a warning: Don't play with God. God is not to be toyed with. He is a force that can and will destroy those who take Him lightly. Remember what He did to Aaron's sons, Nadab and Abihu. He devoured them with fire (Leviticus 10:1-2). I mean, God does not play. There are too many people in the world misleading others, but they are going to pay for their deception. Do you think that God is going to let evil-doers get away with misleading His children? I pity the fool who thinks that God is going to let the Anti Christ, false prophets, and deceivers get away with anything. He is going to destroy them all (Revelation 20:10).

Instead of trying to play with God, we need to let Him use us the way that we're suppose to be used. Let God control your life, and mold you into a powerful soldier. Those who live in God are joint heirs with Christ. They are going to share the kingdom with Him. Those who think that God is a joke are going to suffer the fiery furnace forever. Do you want to be a part of the kingdom, or suffer in the fiery furnace? In the kingdom, there is peace, love, happiness, joy, and eternal life. In the fiery furnace, there is death and suffering. Those who are serious with God are going to inherit the kingdom, so if you want to be a part of that, don't play with God because He is the Ultimate Judge whose judgement you should fear.

DON'T SIT IN THE SEAT OF JUDGMENT

Judge not, that ye be not judged (Matthew 7:1). I know you hear this all the time. It is the Word of God, and it is true. Therefore, my brothers and sisters, don't be judgmental. There is only one God. He is the One who judges all. When He judges, He does it fairly and righteously. That's one of our biggest problems today. Instead of minding our own business and living our lives, we tend to judge others. When you judge others, God will judge you by the same measure. My brothers and sisters, just live your life. God didn't put us down here to judge one another; He put us down here to help each other.

We judge people for many reasons, but God can save that person you judge and that person can be a help to you. That person can join you in helping God save souls. Many of us try to be God. But guess what? God doesn't need your help. He created you. All you have to do is be obedient to Him, and judging others is not one of His commandments. Instead of criticizing those around you, continue to read your Bible and help others get to know God. Each of us has been given a job to do, but the order to be judgmental is not listed among our divine duties.

It is not up to you to judge someone for not living the way that you think that they should live. It is up to that person to make the decision to live the wrong way or the right way. You just continue to do what you are doing for God. You just make sure that you are a faithful servant to Him. The more you judge a person, the more they are going to rebel by continuing to do what they are doing. My brothers and sisters, don't sit in the seat of judgment, because God knows that you don't want anyone judging you.

DON'T WORRY

Why do so many of us continue to put pressure on ourselves? Why do we continue to stress ourselves? Most of all, why do we continue to bug God about our future? God is saying don't worry.

If you will be honest, you will admit that like many Christians, you find yourself worrying about too many things. You worry about everything from when your husband or wife is going to come, to whether or not you are going to be able to make ends meet. It is God's purpose for you to be successful. God will not let you down. My saints and friends, you are going to make it. You are destined to make it; but until you come into all that God has purposed for in your life, you have to stay tough. God loves you because you have a "never say die" attitude. Just relax and allow God to work with you. He knows what you desire to do. He knows what you hunger for. Just follow after Him and He will guide your steps. Don't be anxious, but be patient. God is at work. He's setting everything up for you. Once He places you there, you will be ready. So, be glad and rejoice. In the words of my mother, "Trouble doesn't last always." Don't put trouble on yourself. Don't stress your family. Rely on God. Give all of your burdens to Him.

I'm speaking to you straight from the heart. Ask God to sanctify your mind, body, and soul. Let God prepare you so you don't have to worry about anything. I get fearful, but I ask God to help me. It doesn't feel good walking around with a heart filled with worry. My brothers and sisters, give God everything, and don't take it back. You will find yourself worry free, which is truly what it means to live.

Come unto me, all ye that labor and are heavy laden, and I will give you rest. Take my yoke upon you, and learn of me; for I am meek and lowly in heart: and ye shall find rest unto your souls. For my yoke is easy, and my burden is light (Matthew 11:28-30).

DON'T WORRY ABOUT CROOKED PEOPLE

It seems like everywhere you go, there are crooked people around. I know sometimes you think, "Man, I wish I can be in an environment where people are real." I'm here to tell you not to worry about crooked people because God will handle them. You see, dishonest people have issues, and just because their lives are ruined they want to ruin other people's lives too. They scheme and plot against good people, and sometimes, they even plot against themselves; but God knows how you feel. He knows that you want to be in an environment where you don't have to worry about anyone betraying you, but I'm here to tell you to get over it! His Son, Jesus Christ, was betrayed (Matthew 26:47-56). I know everywhere you go, you feel like the enemy's eyes are watching you. It's sad, but true. Crooked people watch your every move. They are watching even when you think they are not. But wherever you go, hold your head up high. Don't be afraid of those who plot against you; better yet, pray for them. Continue to do well and don't worry about crooked people. The Lord is on your side and He has more power than they do. Though your enemies are watching you, their eyes are no match for God's. His all-seeing eyes are watching their every move, and He knows everything they do, even before they do it.

FULL OF COMPASSION

It's wonderful when you serve the Almighty God, a Lord who blesses you everyday. He shows love to everyone. God is full of compassion. When we sin, He forgives us. When we are alone, He is there to comfort us. I love everything about the Lord. He is an unselfish God. When He blesses me, He blesses my family too. God is so refreshing. He is that fresh spring water that quenches your every thirst. He is that comfortable pillow that soothes and embraces your head. When you are depressed, He gives you joy. God hears your every cry. He answers your every call. He has a remedy for every sickness. When you have a disease, He is your cure. My sisters and brothers, yes, even you who are lying in the hospital bed, He is there right where you are, comforting you and encouraging you to hold on.

In all that you go through, remember to reflect upon His wonderful works and compassion for you. For *He hath made his wonderful works to be remembered: the Lord is gracious and full of compassion* (Psalm 111:4).

GET WITH THE PROGRAM

God is an amazing God. He performs awesome miracles. I just desire to tell you all to get with the program. The program is serving God. Let God program your mind to serve Him. Once God programs your mind to serve Him, you will have the kind of peace which surpasses all understanding (Philippians 4:7).

My brothers and sisters, we are living in the last days, so it's time for us to get right with God. There are many deceivers out there in the world (1 John 2:18-19). There are many false prophets in the world (1 John 4:1). That's why you have to be careful of the people you choose to confide in because they can be misleading you. You have to read the Bible for yourself. You have to get to know God in a more personal way. God is not an evil God; He is a good God. He doesn't bring harm to anyone. He showers His children with love. Put all of your trust in Him. Let God train your mind to live in righteousness. He will not mislead you.

God is the most powerful Prophet in the universe. Everything He says comes to pass. Take heed to His voice. Follow His voice for He is leading you to the way of righteousness. *The steps of a good man are ordered by the Lord: and he delighteth in his way* (Psalm 37:23). Show God that you can endure until the end of time. Get with the program and you will see that there will be a great and eternal reward for you.

GIVE GOD SOME TIME

Let me ask you a question. Why do so many Christians fail to give God some of their time? He is the One who provides them with time. God is the One who blesses them to have time to handle their business. Everyone should give God some of their time.

Give God some time by thanking Him for waking you up in the morning. Every morning, I thank God for blessing me to see another day. It is He that wakes us up each day. While you are taking a break from your studies or from work, that's a good opportunity to meditate on God. Talk to God; His ears are always ready for a conversation.

You can talk to God about anything. He is a friend that understands. He is a friend that will give you His full attention. God will help you understand life because He is life. He will let you know why things happen. Don't just give God time when you are sad or feeling low. Give God some time while things are going well for you. Like I say, I want God to be a part of my everyday life. I want to live with God eternally. Continue to read your Bible, and give God some time because He does hold the world in His hands.

GOD IS ALL THAT MATTERS

I'm just going to get right to the point. God is all that matters. It's not a bad thing to have God continuously on your mind. Those who are in God know that it's a good thing to meditate on Him day and night. God wants you to enjoy life. He wants you to be prosperous and successful, but He wants it to be accomplished within His will. God wants to guide your mind, body and soul. He loves you and wants the best for you, but you have to realize that God is all that matters.

Please don't think God is selfish, arrogant, or stuck on Himself, because He is not. If God was stuck on Himself, He would not think about blessing you. Knowing that God is all that matters is for your benefit. He already knows that He is all that matters. That's why He's in heaven, a place that He also wants you to be. God created mankind to worship Him. He created us to praise and honor Him. Once we realize that, all of us will see that praising God is fun. Not in the sense of playing with Him, but fun as in being happy to praise God because He is in our lives.

Acknowledge God by speaking to your heart through the Spirit. Tell Him that you love Him. Tell others about Him. Give yourself a pat on the back for walking that Christ-like walk, for you realize that God is all that matters.

GOD IS AWESOME

Check this out, my brothers and sisters. God is awesome. Remember and recall the awesomeness of our God, who made a way of escape for those who survived the Twin Towers. Remember and recall the awesomeness of our God in the testimony of those who have survived abusive relationships. Yes, I'm talking about an awesome God. I'm talking about a God who builds His people with strength. During the times that His children are on the verge of fainting, He redeems them with strength. God is a tremendous God. He is the only true God. He makes sure His enemies feel His wrath. God builds His church on the basis of the fruit of the Spirit, which is through His beloved Son, Jesus Christ, our Lord and Savior. And so, if you don't believe that God is awesome, I'm quite sure you will when you remember and recall that it was an awesome God who got you out of trouble. It was an awesome God who helped you get a high school diploma, G.E.D., and all those college degrees that you have mounted on your wall.

It behooves us all to better recognize GOD just for the name He has. His name should tell you that He's awesome. The "G" stands for "Great One." The "O" stands for "Omnipotent." The "D" stands for "Delightment." My brothers and sisters, give God the praises for He is the awesome force that made you in His image.

GOD IS GOING TO WORK IT OUT

Please stop whatever you are doing and relax. Stop pacing back and forth across your room, and please stop worrying your ministers, for God is going to work it out. Whatever you are going through, God is going to work it out. Do you think God is going to leave you in the situation you are in? Do you think God is going to let that problem hinder you? My brothers and sisters, you belong to God. He will not let anything get the best of you. He's going to help you get that job you desire. He's going to help your children graduate from high school and college. He is going to free your relatives from addictions to drugs, alcohol, or cigarettes. Your bills are going to get paid. Your marriage is going to get restored. Your spirit is going to be fulfilled. If I were you, I would be rejoicing, for God is going to take care of everything. Working things out – even the impossible – is simply part of His nature.

GOD IS MIGHTY

Many people don't understand God. God operates in ways that you can't imagine. He makes the weakest men the strongest, and the poorest men the richest. That's why I try not to question God because nothing is impossible for Him to do (Matthew 19:26). God is mighty; He can appear in any form that He chooses. He talked to Moses through a burning bush (Exodus 3:2) and He saved Daniel from the lion's den (Daniel 6:14-28). If I continue to tell you all the miraculous things that God has done, I would be writing the Bible all over again.

You have to understand how mighty God is. I'm talking about the God who rules the kingdom of heaven, and who is offering us an opportunity to dwell with Him. All of us should take advantage of His offer, and meanwhile, meet the challenges of Satan head on because Satan is going to try to set a pit for us to fall in. But the amazing part about serving the Lord is that He won't allow you to fall in the pit. And so, everyone should be ready to jump on the bandwagon to sojourn to heaven. God can just snap His finger, and Satan would be destroyed. Satan knows his time is almost up; that's why he's trying his best to bring down more people with him. God loves everyone, and He blesses those who try their best to serve Him. He also keeps His promises. Every time you see a rainbow, it is a reminder that God will keep His promise that He won't destroy the world with a flood (Genesis 9:8-16). Most importantly, why do I say God is mighty? Of all the evil things that go on in this world, it takes a mighty force to hold it up. To those who choose not to honor God: beware! That same mighty force is going to destroy all evil-doers.

GOD IS WORTHY

Children of God, our Father is worthy to be praised. If it weren't for Him, we wouldn't exist. God is the One who has all the power. He created heaven and earth. To Him, we should give all glory and honor. His throne is in heaven where His Son, Jesus Christ, sits on the right hand side of Him (Hebrews 8:1). God is able to conquer all things. He gave His children the power to conquer all things. He is always there to meet His children's needs. He is a great Father.

If people would only forget about themselves, and stay focused on God, the world would be a peaceful place. Our Father dwells in peace. He is peace. That's what He wants all us to have. People, stop being selfish and bless the Lord. When you need a blessing, He blesses you; so why can't you bless Him? It's so sad the way people get caught up in themselves as if they are in control of things. Everything belongs to God, and not man. God blessed you to be the boss at your job. He blessed you to be the C.E.O. at a company, so don't lose sight of the One who is really in charge and forget about Him. God has the richest kingdom in the universe and we all have a place in His kingdom because He loves all of us. Therefore, you should worship Him for He is worthy.

GOD KNOWS HOW YOU ARE FEELING

How are you doing, my friends? I'm here to tell you that God knows how you are feeling. God is a searcher of hearts. He knows when you are happy, or sad. He knows how you feel when you lose a loved one. He knows how you feel when you get a car. God knows how you feel when you graduate. He knows everything. Whatever you do my friends, don't let anything drive you crazy. Give all of your worries to God. You can't do everything by yourself. God is a Father who is willing to help you. He will never neglect you. When you are down, He will be there to lift you up. When you are crying, He will be there to dry your tears. When you are lonely, He will be there to keep you company. Never think that God is not present because He is the first One, and the main Source that always knows how you are feeling.

GOD KNOWS WHAT'S BEST

Many people try to do things on their own. They just don't know that God will bless them with anything their heart desired. God knows what's best for all of us. He was the One who created us, and if He created us, common sense should tell us that He knows what's best for us.
God knows what kind of car your heart desires. He knows what kind of house your heart desires. He knows how much money your heart desires. God even knows what kind of spouse your heart desires. He knows everything about you. Just wait on Him and He will provide you with all of these things. However, you have to work hard for everything that you want. You have to earn it. There are going to be trials and tribulations. It is up to you to stand tall during your hard times. Everything is not going to be easy because Satan is going to ease his way on in, but you can't let him get the best of you. Once you place your faith in God, and hold on to Him, He is going to bless you with everything according to His will. He is going to bless you to be successful and prosperous, because He knows what's best for you.

GOD'S LITTLE LAMBS

God's Little Lambs is a place where your children will be nurtured. It is a place where your children will have fun. God's Little Lambs is a place where your kids will have a good upbringing. It is a place where you don't have to worry about them being in any danger. It is a place where your children will receive the proper care. God's Little Lambs is a place where the Almighty God dwells, so don't worry about anything because His most loyal servants will take care of them.

For my sister, **Z.D.**

GOD SEES THE LIGHT IN YOU

I know something that you may not know. God sees the light in you. Do you know why God sees the light in you? He sees it because He is that light. God knows Himself and He loves Himself; and in God, there is no darkness. Even if the sun never shines and the moon never rises, in God, there still will be no darkness. Knowing that God's light shines, and it does shine, means that your light shines too, because He lives in you. Do you understand where I'm coming from? God loves you so much that He is willing to live in you. Now that is something to shout about. Nothing can put out that light and nothing can overtake that light which shines in you. That dynamic light feeds off of the Word of God. That dynamic light feeds off of love. That dynamic light feeds off of doing good. Everywhere you go that light shines in you. Even when you die, that light is going to shine in you. Just like when Moses died, the light was still shining in him (Deuteronomy 34:7). Rise up and know that God sees the light in you, and be happy for that light is greater than darkness.

GOD UNDERSTANDS

My brothers and sisters, don't be depressed because of what you are going through, and don't be down about your circumstances or situations. God is with you. He hasn't left you. God understands your time of tribulation. Just because you are not at the place you want to be, doesn't mean that God is angry with you. Don't get frustrated and don't be weary. God has a plan set for you. There was a time when I felt the same way that you are feeling. God knows all about it, and right now, at this very moment, He's saying your life is not over. He's not done with you. He understands how you feel. At this very moment, God is saying stop crying and complaining. He's saying that He has to prepare you. He understands that you may not be feeling good about yourself. He understands that you may feel guilty over what you have done. God does not hate you. He wants the best for you.

Stop being hard on yourself. Love yourself and start back taking care of yourself. Open your heart to Christ, and invite Him in. I know you may feel that you've disappointed Him and are afraid that you may do it again. But don't worry. He will be there to pick you up.

I was in the same position that you are in. I felt like I let God down. I wouldn't forgive myself because I felt in my heart that I had disappointed God. I felt as though I didn't deserve His forgiveness. Just know this: God understands what you are going through. He loves you and He wants the best for you. He has not forgotten about you so what you need to do is talk to Christ Jesus. Ask Him for His help so He can aid you in reaching your destiny.

Last, but not least; stop feeling guilty and being hard on yourself. Don't speak negatively about yourself. Get into a relationship with the Holy Trinity and remember that God always understands what you are going through.

HANDLE YOUR BUSINESS

Can I get real with you? Why are you still holding yourself back? You have a lot of things to accomplish, so get off of your behind. God does not want you sitting on your behind; He wants you to handle your business. God knows that you love Him. He knows that you want to serve Him, but you can't serve Him sitting down and doing nothing. Get out there and get a job or go to school. There are plenty of areas where He wants to use you, and being in the bed is not one of them. There are people out there waiting to see you. They need your help. Don't think about yourself, but think about those who need you. God wants to use you to help them.

My brothers and sisters, know that you can make it. Know that you can do all things through Christ which strengthens you (Philippians 4:13). My brothers and sisters, God wants you. He's reaching out to you. He's calling on you. Look at the world today. The enemy is destroying everyone that he can. You are that soldier that God is ready to prepare. There is always room for help. There is plenty of space in heaven. God has a spot open for you. You don't have to be perfect to go to heaven. Don't say that you are not good enough. That's only an excuse for you to stay in bed. Don't be afraid that you are not going to make it. Say in your heart, "With God's help, I'm going to make it; and it's time for me to handle my business."

HOLD YOUR HEAD UP

How are you doing, my wonderful saints and friends? It feels so good to serve the Almighty God. He is the One who uplifts our spirits. The Lord is good to all. I just want to tell you all to hold your head up. There should be no saint holding his or her head down. God loves all of us. His grace is upon all of His children. Whenever we slip, He will be there to pick us up. Whenever we fall into a pit, God will be there to get us out.

Love God with your whole heart. Don't put anyone before Him (Exodus 20:3). God will never leave or forsake you. He is with you even when you think He's not. Continue to walk boldly in faith. Remember that God is right by your side. Have faith in the Lord and know that you can't be brought down. Don't let the enemy come and take your joy. Don't let the enemy come and take your confidence. *No weapon form against you shall prosper* (Isaiah 54:17). God has given us the power to tread over the enemy (Luke 10:19). It is up to us to use it. Hold your head up high and let people know that you are more than a conqueror (Romans 8:37).

I DARE YOU

It is funny how some people walk around thinking that they rule the earth, and thinking that they own everything, as if they are God. Those types of people need to wake up from whatever dream they are having. It is the Almighty God who rules over everything. It is the Almighty God who owns everything. He put His breath in your body so you can live. I dare anyone to say that God doesn't exist. Who created the solar system? Man didn't do it. God created everything with His power and majesty (Genesis 1). God is a mighty force that no one can defeat. He is a force that can wipe out any army. He holds the world in His hands. I dare anyone to test God. I dare anyone to challenge God. There is no test or challenge too hard for Him. He will look at us and laugh. Anyone who thinks that he or she is perfect should show God that he or she is mightier than Him. Otherwise, be quiet!

IT'S ALL ABOUT GOD

My friends, open your mouths and say, "It's all about God." God is the great One. He created you from the dust of the earth. He knows everything about you. God is the greatest craftsman in the universe. Look at the trees, the sky, the oceans, and the solar system. God created them all. When it comes to His children, He nurtures them. God doesn't leave His children weak. He gives them strength, knowledge, wisdom, love, joy, and peace. He blesses His children daily. He feeds the earth with His rain. God is an unselfish God. The earth cries out to Him, and He shields it. He is the protector of us all. God's blessings are everlasting. His love for us is everlasting. Whenever you get noticed for doing something marvelous, just remember it's not about you; it's all about the Almighty and Trustworthy God.

IT'S TIME OUT FOR GETTING USED

Check this out, my brothers and sisters, I know we are caring people, but it's time out for us getting used. God doesn't want anyone to use us, therefore, we don't have to take getting used. Some people will abuse and misuse your kindness. You try to be so kind and generous to them, but they use it to their advantage. I know you are sick and tired of getting used. God said don't allow anyone to take your kindness for granted. I'm getting tired of us Christians and saints of the Lord getting used. We welcome people into our homes and hearts and they try to take advantage of us. They try to tear our homes and hearts apart. It's time out for that. My brothers and sisters, don't allow anyone to use you. You can be nice and kind to those types of people, but stop allowing them to manipulate you.

When it comes to a relationship, be on guard. That person that you think is for you may be against you. That person may try to suck you dry, so be careful. That's why Paul teaches us to *Be not unequally yoked together with unbelievers: for what fellowship hath righteousness with unrighteousness? And what communion hath light with darkness?* (2 Corinthians 6:14). The Lord loves His children and He doesn't want any of us to get hurt or be used. The Lord doesn't want any of us to get our heart broken. That's why He gave us discernment. Getting used is a serious thing because your heart is involved in it. We have to stop allowing people to take advantage of us. They don't care about us. If they cared about us, they would not use us. You have people out there who are unwilling to show you that they care about you. They don't make any efforts. My Christian saints and friends, let us keep our discernment alert systems on, and watch out for those who try to use us because it is time for it to stop.

JUST ASK SOMEBODY

The Lord shines His light on His children daily. He gives His children peace. He absolutely blesses those who are faithful to Him. Why not serve God? Didn't He put breath in your body? Let me also clarify that it wasn't simply breath, but it was His own breath. God is the One who provides for you. He is the One who shelters you. Therefore, study to show thyself approved unto Him (2 Timothy 2:15), place no limit on yourself, and keep striving for success. Know that you can't be stop. With the Lord on your side, who can stop you? It's the same as saying, *If God is for me who can be against me?* (Romans 8:31). Continue to believe in God. Keep Him in your heart. He is worthy to be praised. And know this, by the way you walk, people will know that there is something special about you. By the way you talk, people will know that Christ's light shines in you because His light is a detection signal. Don't worry; you will know your enemies because they will scatter when they see the light. They can't handle that light that shines in you. His light is brighter than the sun. Just ask somebody. And I'm not talking about just anybody, but a believer in the Almighty God.

KEY TO SUCCESS

We all have goals that we desire to accomplish or dreams we hope will someday come true. And everyday, we work hard to reach that goal. And so, I want you to know that we all have the power to be successful. Yes, I'm writing to tell you that with God, you can become successful because He is the key to success. God will be there to guide you through your struggles, *for this God is our God forever and ever: he will be our guide even unto death* (Psalm 48:14). God will not lead you astray. He will be with you every step of the way for *the steps of a good man are ordered by the Lord: and he delighteth in his way* (Psalm 37:23).

When you study for a test, He will be there to help you. When you train, He will be your coach. When you are at a job interview, He will be your confidence. God will be anything that you ask Him to be except evil. He just wants you to have faith in Him with your whole heart. God will open the door of opportunity for you to become successful, and that's why I say He is the key to success.

LET GOD DIRECT YOUR MIND

Today is a beautiful day that the Almighty God has created. Our God is an awesome God. He is a unique God. Always remember that God cares about you, and because of that, my friends, let Him direct your mind. All He wants to do is lead you the right way. *I will instruct thee and teach thee in the way which thou shalt go: I will guide thee with mine eye* (Psalm 32:8). God desires to and will be your favorite teacher if you would just pay attention to Him and heed His instruction. Give God your full attention. In His class, you won't get bored because He will keep you smiling, and interested, for He is a great motivational speaker. God will shower you with joy. He will shower you with blessings. God will show you things that you've never seen before. Keep pressing in the direction of God and it is there that you will find success. Everywhere you go, God will shine His light upon you. Others will recognize that there is something special about you. When God directs your mind, you will make the right decisions. When God directs your mind, you will make great decisions. For our God is a great guidance counselor. With my whole heart, I encourage you to let God direct your mind.

LIFT UP YOUR HANDS

We should all give praises to God for being in our lives. Look at all of the wonderful things that He does for us. He blesses us to be healthy, and with clothes on our backs. He blesses us with shelter and transportation. God deserves all of the praises, and blessings from us, therefore, we need to lift up our hands to Him. When it comes to His children, God does not hesitate to meet our every need. He knows what our hearts desire. As long as you bless God, He is going to continue to bless you.

He is a loving God. Sometimes words can't describe how great He is. God is that tree that gives you shade when it's too hot outside. He is that friend who helps you study. God is that star that shines the brightest. He is that map that gives you guidance, so you can head in the right direction. And so, don't take God for granted because He doesn't play any games. He is real, a force that can blow you away. For His power and might alone, He is worthy of all praises. In everything you do, lift up your hands, acknowledge Him because He loves being the center of attention. Lift up your hands, for He is the One that is going to help you make it to the top of the ladder. Rejoice, and lift up your hands unto our God, Alpha and Omega, now and forever!

LIVE TO BLESS GOD

Wow; what a fantastic day the Almighty God has created! It takes an awesome King to create such an awesome day. My brothers and sisters, let's just live to bless God. Why do I say live to bless God? Because He was kind enough to create you. He spent His precious time planning out how wonderful He wanted you to be; and you know what? He did a good job creating you. He did not make any flaws creating you. The beautiful earth that you and I live on, He created it (Genesis 1). The oceans that surfers surf upon, God created them. The solar system that scientists explore, God created it. And so, if I were you, I would be praising God. If I were you, I would be honoring Him. Look how beautiful God made your wife. Look how handsome God made your husband. Look how precious He made your children. Must I continue to urge you to live to bless God: the One who sent His beloved Son to die for you, the One who cured you from all of your infirmities? And so, no; it would not hurt you to open your Bible, and read it. Get closer to God so you can truly adore Him. Live to bless God, all you creatures here below. Bless the Lord at all times for He is the One who smiles down upon you with joy.

LOVE ONE ANOTHER

Hello to everyone that's on this great planet that God created. God did a great job creating Earth. He created and positioned everything in such a remarkable way. I love and thank God for creating such a beautiful planet because, my friends, everything was crafted with such love and care. Simply put, we should love one another for God created us out of love, and wants us to love, not hate, each other. Therefore, forgive those who trespass against you. When you love your enemies, it lets God know that you have a caring heart. It lets God know that you don't let hate control your heart. And for those of you who have hate in your heart or an angry spirit, take it to Jesus Christ and He will take it away from you.

Jesus Christ doesn't want anyone walking around with a hateful heart. He searches everyone's hearts to make sure that they have love in it. Like I always say, I love God Almighty and I thank Him for Jesus Christ for He is real and His love is genuine. Where you find Jesus Christ, you find love. Where there is a close family, there is Jesus Christ. My brothers and sisters, let's show love toward each other, for we are joint heirs of Christ: one big happy family. You might as well get used to loving one another and showing love down here on earth, because when you go to heaven you're not going to have a problem doing it.

Love one another, my brothers and sisters. It makes your Heavenly Father proud of creating you; it makes Jesus Christ smile because you are one of His joint heirs, and it fills Abraham with joy that you were one of the stars that God told him to look upon (Genesis 15:5-6). Amen.

LOVE WHAT YOU DO FOR GOD

Please hear me out on this one, my brothers and sisters. You must love what you do for God. Loving what you do for the Lord lets Him know that you appreciate Him. It lets Him know that you care about serving Him. It also lets God know that you are not ashamed of what you do. I don't care if it's mopping the floor, vacuuming rugs, cleaning windows or painting walls; love what you do for God. When your Heavenly Father sees that you love what you do for Him, He will enhance your talent and let people see the great works that you do for Him. I know God loves His ministers who submit to His will for their lives. It lets Him know that they are not disobedient. It lets Him know that they love Him. The best part about it is that God's true ministers will gladly tell you that they don't do what they do for money or other material gain, but they do it because they love Him. When God rewards those who love what they do for Him, don't hate. They have sweated, cried, and put hard work into what they do. Love what you do for God, embrace it, and be proud of what you do, for it lets God know that the works you do for Him are remarkable in His and His Son's eyes.

P.S. God does not hate what He does for you. He loves it.

LOVE YOURSELF

Let me ask you a question. How can you love others if you don't love yourself? You've got to have love in order to give love. Many people today look for man to give them love instead of looking for love from the true source. When you love God, you love yourself for He is in you. Before you look to others to give you love, look to God. God loves you more than anybody. God loves you more than you love yourself. God loves you with a passion. No matter how many times you do wrong, He still loves you. Even when you put Him on a shelf, He still loves you. He loves you no matter what you do.

And so, I invite you to take a look at your reflection in the mirror and say that you love yourself. Treat yourself with kindness. Shower yourself with adoration. Be happy about yourself. Be willing to love yourself because if there is no one around to give you love what are you going to do? That's why self-love is so important. There is no guarantee that people are going to love you. Always remember that Jesus loves you and yes, we know this for the Bible tells all of us so. And on this note, my dear friends, when you wake up each day, give yourself a big hug and say, "I love me." Keep your eyes on God, and all His love will shine upon you.

MASTER OF THE UNIVERSE

Read this very carefully. Some people go from place to place, not knowing who God is. Some people don't have God in their minds. There are people who have heard of Him, but refuse to get to know Him. There are people who know Him, but refuse to praise Him because they are upset with Him. I'm here to tell you that God is the Master of the universe. God created all things. He created the entire solar system. Man did not create anything. Satan did not create anything. These other gods that many people serve don't have power to create anything.

God is so magnificent. All He did was open His mouth and the earth was created (Genesis 1). His throne is in heaven where He and His Son dwell. God keeps His eyes on the earth. He watches everyone's comings and goings. God is the most powerful force in the universe. He can't be destroyed. When He speaks, mountains tremble. Although He is mighty, God doesn't want you to run away from Him. He wants you to praise and worship Him. God is not a monster; He is our Lord and Savior. He is a loving and caring Father. It is amazing the way the stars, sun, moon, and the clouds obey Him. How many people do you know who can control the universe? None but the Almighty God because He is the Master of it.

MOVE SWIFTLY

Hurry, get up, and move before you miss your blessings. My brothers and sisters, you have to move swiftly for God. When God tells you to feed the poor, go do it. It pleases God when His children do something for those less fortunate. God is not a slow mover and He doesn't want His children to be slothful either. As quickly as you blink your eyes, God can bless you with an automobile, a spouse, a home, children and riches. It just sickens me when people say that God is slow. The truth is that they are just not patient enough to wait on Him.

Just like you want your blessings to come quickly, God wants you to make haste for Him. God has all of your blessings in His hands. When it comes to blessing you, He is not going to close His hands as long as you are obedient to Him. Prove to God that you are willing to serve Him. Show God that you are a faithful servant. Believe me, He is going to test you. He is going to challenge you to see if you truly love Him. Move swiftly for God. Honor, trust, and adore Him for He is the Holy King. When you stand firm for God, it impresses Him. It makes Him feel good when you praise Him. I love God because even with the many praises He receives, He doesn't brag, boast, or get arrogant. He is a force that is worthy to be honored, so move swiftly for God so He can bless you.

MY FAMILY

I thank God for my family because we are strong. I put so much emphasis on my family because each one of us is independent. It's all because of Elder Betty Gates, my loving mother. When she committed her life to God, we committed our lives to God. The apple doesn't fall far from the tree. Elder Betty Gates planted a seed and God poured down His rain and grew a strong family tree. God is that tree and each one of us are His branches. That's why when a storm passes, the tree never gets knocked down because it is held up by the Almighty God.

So many families in the world are separated because they don't have God in their lives. Without God, your family cannot make it. God will be there to shield and protect you. God will give your family peace, love, happiness, joy, and finances. Satan will give you money also, but it would only be temporary. With God, gifts are everlasting. He will make things easier for you. All you have to do is commit your life to God, fear Him, be patient, and have faith. God will open the doors of the kingdom of heaven and give you what your heart desires.

OBEY THE LORD

It's true; the Lord is good to all. He is an amazing force. God is the epitome of perfection, that's why you need to obey Him. God wants you to be obedient so you can live eternally with Him. He is not trying to prevent you from having fun. He just wants you to abide with Him. When you obey the Lord, your spirit is free. When you obey the Lord, He will grant you anything you need. Just ask Him, and you will receive it. God is not selfish. Believe me, He will bless you. Let your mind and heart dwell with God. That is the best feeling that you can ever have. God is your guide to eternal happiness. I know that you are getting sick and tired of worrying about paying bills, feeling pain, and getting hurt. Put your life in God's hands. Trust me, you won't be disappointed. It will be the best decision you have made in your life. You will not only be successful on earth, but you will also be successful in heaven, and that is the greatest reward that you can ever receive. Obey the Lord for He is the top God.

PLEASE DON'T HATE GOD

Please don't hate God. Why? Because He loves you. God loves you so much that He sent His only begotten Son, Jesus Christ ,down here on earth to die for your sins (John 3:16). God wants you to go to heaven. He wants everything to work out for you. He doesn't want you to get confused or frustrated about what's going on in your life. He doesn't want you to get angry, but if you do, don't let the sun go down upon your wrath (Ephesians 4:26). You see, my brothers and sisters, God is working out something big for you, so praise His holy name. Continue to do well. Continue to help out your fellow neighbors. Know Jesus Christ is real. God is the One who loves you the most. He is the One who is going to see you through. Just knowing that God is planning out everything for you should fill you with gladness. Knowing that God has His eyes set upon you should fill you with gladness. You are a joint heir with Christ. You are precious in God's sight so rejoice, be glad in the Lord, and please don't hate God for He loves you.

PLEASE DON'T PUT GOD ON A SHELF

Stop what you are doing right now and listen to what the Spirit of the Lord is saying. He's saying please don't put God on a shelf. Why would you want to put someone on a shelf that is always there for you? God does not want to be on your dusty shelf. He does not belong on your dusty shelf. He is the One who helps you during your good times and bad times. My brothers and sisters, you need God at all times. Even when you make it to the top of the ladder, you still need Him. In fact, that's the time you really need Him.

When you were crying in the midnight hour, God was the One who told you everything is going to be all right. When everyone was harassing you and calling you out your name, God was there to dry your tears. All of a sudden, the enemy wants to make us believe that we can put the Almighty on a shelf. God is not a record that we dust off and play at our leisure. He is rich in all of His glory. When things don't work out for us, that's the time we want to call on Him. But we should bless Him at all times.

Keep God off of your shelf. He loves being recognized. He appreciates it when you acknowledge His existence. In everything you accomplish, and even in the things you don't accomplish, give God the glory because He will always find a way to work things out. It is good to praise God at all times, so please don't put Him on a shelf.

PLEASE DON'T REJECT GOD

This is a message that I'm delivering to you from way deep down in my soul. My brothers and sisters, please don't reject God because rejecting God is not a good thing to do. My brothers and sisters, don't reject a force whose love for you surpasses the love of man. God is here to show you guidance. He is here to help you get through life. Accept God more and more in your life. You need Him for everything. When you reject God, you are saying that you don't need Him. Face it; you are not going to make it without God. You can't handle everything by yourself. Put God in your life and let Him take full control of your life. He loves you. He will never reject you. All He is doing is waiting on you. He is waiting on you to ask for His help. He is waiting on you to call on Him. God knows when you have been sinning, but He will not reject you for doing that. He knows your heart and He is graceful and loving enough to forgive you. He will not hurt you because He knows that you are not perfect. We all have sinned. We all have been down the pathway of wrongdoing.

There is no excuse for rejecting God. Doing such a thing is worse than drug abuse. Rejecting God is worse than working for the enemy. Don't reject God because you think that you don't deserve His goodness. No one deserves the goodness of the Lord, but He forgives us anyway. God cleans us and makes us whiter than snow so we can be holy like Him. Accept God with everything that you have and with everything that you are going through. His light will shine through you each step of the way. My brothers and sisters, man will reject you, but God won't, so please don't reject Him.

PLEASE DON'T TAKE YOUR EYES OFF OF GOD

My Christian saints and friends, please don't take your eyes off of God. Taking your eyes off God is like walking with a blindfold on your eyes. You may think that you can make it without guidance. If so, you are only fooling yourself. Keep your eyes on God because the enemy is creeping up on you. The enemy is waiting for you to slip. He wants you to lean on your own understanding. Don't try to guide yourself; let God guide you. When we guide ourselves, we can easily stumble and fall, but with God guiding us, we continue to stand. With God guiding us, we won't fall into temptation. The second you take your eyes off God, the enemy jumps up on you.

My brothers and sisters, that's the enemy's job. You are very dangerous to the enemy. I'm telling you to keep your eyes on God, so you don't have to worry about the adversary overwhelming you. When you keep your eyes on God, you are spiritually acknowledging Him. When you keep your eyes on God, you are showing Him that you recognize His existence. When you keep your eyes on God, you are allowing Him to guide you. Let God know that He's on your mind. Let God know that you appreciate Him for being everywhere you go. My Christian saints and friends, keep your eyes on God, for the pathway of righteousness will be clearly set for you.

PLEASE GOD

How are you doing, my brothers and sisters? I'm doing great. I just want to admonish you to live to please God. God is the One who watches everything. He watches your every going. And I know that right about now, you may be saying to yourself, "I must be perfect since God watches my every move." Not true. But God knows that avoiding sin is not simple. After all, we live in a sinful world. That's why through His Son, Jesus Christ, sin was defeated, and God gives us abundant grace and mercy.

God is a merciful King. He is a God of comfort, therefore, let us please Him. Please God by trusting in Him. He won't mislead you. He won't break your heart. He is a force that does marvelous works. Please God by opening your heart to others. That lets Him know that you care about your neighbors. The more you open your heart to those around you, the more your blessings come down. Love God with your whole heart. Let God take full control of your life. When God is in control, nothing can stop you from reaching your destiny. Live to please God for it shows that you are willing to go and stay on the right path.

PUT GOD FIRST

Let me ask you a question. Does God come first in your life? If He doesn't, it's time for you to put Him first. God doesn't like being second, third, fourth, or fifth. He likes being first. God is a jealous God; He commanded us not to put anything before Him (Exodus 20:3). He has the right to be jealous because He created us, yet, at times, we have the nerve to put things before Him. Many times, we put our houses before God, our cars, and our jobs before Him. He is the One who made the way for us to get those things. When we put God first, watch how many blessings pour down on us.

Whatever you do, my fellow servant of God, acknowledge the Lord. Let Him know that you appreciate Him. Don't take Him for granted. Keep your mind focused on Him. Open up your heart to Him. God is the richest source in the universe. He can provide you with anything you want. All you have to do is obey His commandments. God is not a monster. He won't do anything to hurt or harm you. My friends, just put God first in your life, and keep Him first.

RECOGNIZE GOD

It's pathetic how people cry when they don't receive any attention. Some people actually think that the world revolves around them. Well, I'm going to offer a reality check. The world doesn't revolve around any mortal man; it revolves around the Almighty God.

Everyone needs to recognize God. How do you think the solar system operates? How do you think it rains? How do you think the days change? It all happens because of the Almighty God. *Be still, and know that I am God* (Psalm 46:10). It was God who created the earth. It was God who created the solar system. God is perfect in everything He does. God doesn't make any mistakes. Many try to figure Him out, but don't get anywhere. He can't be figured out. Just continue to ask God for more wisdom and understanding. Anything you want to know, God will tell you. He is a faithful and just Father. God will leave you amazed by the works He displays. He is an awesome God! Who helps you get out of tough situations? Who helped you pass that class that was giving you problems? The Almighty God did. People, just recognize God, and may peace be with you.

REFUSE TO BE ABUSED

Listen to me very carefully, my brothers and sisters; refuse to be abused. I'm speaking to you with an open heart. Refuse to let anyone mentally, physically, or spiritually abuse you. When someone abuses you in any manner, it's not love. Women often say, "He beats me because he loves me." That is a lie. Don't let any man lay his hand on you in a violent manner. True love is godly love. If someone loves you, he or she will not physically abuse you.

In addition, don't let anyone mentally abuse you either. There are many people in bondage because of mental abuses. They are afraid to step out in faith due to someone exploiting their mind. Someone may have told them that they are not going to amount to anything. Someone may have constantly cursed them out. Regardless to whether it's your parents, schoolteacher, or spouse; don't let anyone mentally abuse you.

Moreover, don't let anyone spiritually abuse you. I hate when people get spiritually battered. Don't let anyone steal your peace, joy, happiness, kindness, hope, patience, and love. When they do that, they are spiritually robbing you. My brothers and sisters, stick to Jesus Christ, He will never do those things to you. He will not mentally, physically, or spiritually mistreat you. He gives you real deal love, the type of love that you don't have to beg for. My brothers and sisters, refuse to be abused for abuse is the fuse of lifelong fear and bondage.

SHARE YOUR GIFT

It's wonderful when you have good health. When you have the ability to move around. The strength to endure things. The Almighty God anoints you to have those things. As your brother, I'm asking you to share your gift that the Almighty God gave you. If the Almighty God granted you the gift to sing, you should sing. If He granted you the gift to write, you should write. If God granted you the gift to preach, you should preach. You will be surprised with how many lives you touch with your gift.

When God endows you with something, He wants you to use it. When God grants you with something, He doesn't make any mistakes. He is sharing His power with you. Now, if God can share His power with you, you can share your gift with others. God granted you the gift, and He expects you to share it. Don't let your gift be in vain. Don't let it go to waste. It's not all about you. It's all about God. God does not want you to be selfish; He wants you to be like Him, so be generous and share your gift.

SHOW GOD LOVE

What's going on, my brothers and sisters? How are you all doing? I'm doing just fine. I just want to tell you all to show God love. He shows you love, and He takes great care of those who show Him love. He preserves those who love Him. When you feel like nothing is going to happen for you, just hold on and know that God is going to make a way for you. All God wants you to do is continue to believe in Him. It is for your own good. God will bless you with anything that your heart desires. He will help you climb that mountain all the way to the top.

But seek ye first the kingdom of God, and his righteousness; and all these things shall be added unto you (Matthew 6:33). God doesn't deal with unbelievers; He deals with believers. Give God the glory each day when you awake. Praise God for blessing you to be a beautiful creature. Everything that God created is beautiful. He doesn't dwell with ugliness. He is a God of great kindness. He is a God with everlasting love. Show God love. Besides, He shows you love.

SPEAK POSITIVE

The journey of life would be much easier if we spoke positive to each other and ourselves. There are many people today speaking negative to each other. Why do we speak negative? Is the God that created us negative? He is nowhere near negative. In the first chapter of the Book of Genesis, I recall God Almighty saying everything He created is good. God did not speak bad things about what He created. Why can't we be the same way? Why can't we speak positive like God does? He wants us to speak good things.

This Christian journey is difficult enough for us, but we make it even harder when we speak negative toward each other. Don't pour negative words in your sisters' and brothers' spirits; pour positive. God wants each and every last one of us to speak encouragement to each other. With all the evil that's going on in this world, we all need positive reinforcement in order to fight against it. Nothing is going to change unless we change. Speak positive, live positive, and be positive, for the world that God created is awesome. It can be even more spectacular if everyone who is dwelling in it would just love one another.

STAY DEEP IN GOD

Hello, my wonderful brothers and sisters in Christ Jesus. I just want to tell you all to stay deep in God. God is the One who reveals all things. He is the One who searches the depths of our souls. Meditate on God and speak deeply to Him. Tell God how you feel about Him. Submit yourself to Him. Tell God how much you love Him. While you are living, get to know Him more and more. Let His light shine upon you.

I'm praying that we all continue to get closer to God, so we can see His face. We all need Him. God is the One who uplifts our spirits. He is the One who motivates us. Allow God to clean you. He will not leave you filthy. As you get deep in God, He will bless you to become powerful. As you get deep in God, He will reveal things to you. I love God and I need Him everyday, every hour, every minute, and every second of my life. God is the One who is going to increase every area of your life. From now on, let us continue to stay focused on God, Jesus Christ, and the Holy Spirit. Let us stay committed to the Holy Trinity.

(Pray with me) "Father, God bless us to continue to stay focused on You and the promises that You have for us. We know that as long as we continue to stay focused on You, we are going to receive those things that You promised us. So, Father God, continue to enlighten us because we can't live without You." And on that note, my brothers and sisters, we (myself included) have to stay deep in God because He is all that matters.

STAY HAPPY

Some people think that just because they are unhappy that you supposed to be unhappy. They try their best to make you feel the same way. My brothers and sisters, don't feed into it. Instead, continue to stay happy. God blesses you with joy, so don't let anyone or anything take it away from you. He is an awesome God. Every place that you go, let your light shine.

Don't be concerned about what people say to you. You have something that they don't understand. You have something that they are searching for. They just don't know what trials and tribulations you go through. People are always quick to judge and assume the worse, but don't let that get you down. Just keep seeking after God's righteousness. No one but God has a place to put you when you die. Serve God with hope. Serve God, for He is worthy to be praised. If God blesses you with happiness, why should you worry about what people say about you? If they don't care about being happy, so what? You just continue to stay joyful because your Heavenly Father granted you with happiness.

STAY IN TOUCH WITH GOD

It is so tremendous to have the Great and Almighty God in your life. As a matter of fact, there is nothing better. My brothers and sisters, if you have God Almighty in your life, make sure you stay in touch with Him. You stay in touch with Him by reading your Bible. You stay in touch with Him by praying. You stay in touch with Him by going to church, Bible class, listening to gospel radio, and by watching the gospel programming as it goes forth on television.

For those of you who don't have God in your life, get Him into your life. He is not hard to find. Believe it or not, He is right there with you. He is a God who loves you and will love you better than anyone or anything else. He is a God who is full of compassion. He is a God who is right there with you when you are hurt. He is God who is right there with you when you fall. Once you get Him into your life, stay in touch with Him. My brothers and sisters, you can't breathe without God and you can't survive without Him, so be glad that you accepted Him into your life and make sure you stay in touch with Him.

STRAIGHT FROM THE HEART

Do me a favor, and stop thinking about yourself for a moment. Think about those who don't have a place to stay. Think about those who don't know when their next meal is coming. Do you see how blessed you are? Do you know how blessed you are? It is fortunate that you have a place to stay. Thank God Almighty that you have a place to call home. Jesus Christ has chosen me to get this message across to you. Don't just think about yourself, but consider others. I'm guilty of being selfish. There are many starving people in the world, and that's why it's our mission to help them. We are not only going to help those in America, but also those in other countries, with the help of God.

Everyone should have that same attitude. There is a nation out there that is waiting for each of us to reach out to them. When you are eating your home cooked meal, think about that child who is hungry in Africa. Next time you buy some expensive clothes, think about that child in Russia who is wearing rags. Imagine what it's like being in their shoes. You may struggle, but there are some individuals who struggles more than you do. There are some individuals who have no choice, but to struggle. I'm praying that God cleans out all the selfishness, not only in me, but also in you, so we can complete the mission that He desires us to. My brothers and sisters, thank you for this moment we've shared, and know that I'm speaking to you straight from the heart.

TAKE HEED

Hold up for me right quick! Please listen to the words that I'm about to say. Do yourself a big favor and open up your heart to God. Once you do that, you will feel great. Opening up your heart to God is a huge relief. It's a huge relief from pressure and stress. You will find out that God truly loves you. You might have heard about the love that God has, but once you open up your heart, you will find out that it's really true. My brothers and sisters, God loves you with a passion. He loves you so much that He sent His only begotten Son to earth to be sacrificed for your sins. Let this marinate in your mind: who will be willing to die for you? God must really love you if He sent His only Son to die for you. What man on earth will sacrifice his child for you? What man on earth will die for you? Give your life to God. No other love is greater.

God will comfort you all the day long. He's reaching His arms out to you. God will motivate, guide, heal, and bless you. At this very hour, open up your heart to God and accept His only begotten Son, Jesus Christ, as your personal Savior. As soon as you do this, you will realize the wonderful destiny He has set out for you. You will find out that Jesus Christ is a loving, remarkable, real, sensational, and cool Savior. Jesus Christ is the total package, and in that package comes love, happiness, joy, gentleness, compassion, comfort, life more abundantly, hope, success and eternal life. My brothers and sisters, please open up your hearts to God and take heed to what He tells you.

THE GENERATOR OF MOTIVATION

God is the generator of motivation. He blesses all of His children with confidence. If we are weak, He blesses us to be strong. A strong mind is more powerful than a strong body. God gives us the will power to make it through any trial or tribulation. He gives us the extra push to make it to the top. *In my distress I cried unto the Lord, and he heard me* (Psalm 120:1). God will hear your every cry. He will never forsake you. He loves all of us.

Never lose sight of God. You can't make it through life without Him. God is not here to put harm on you. He just wants you to serve Him. And watch how all your blessings come in the time you start serving God. God will protect you from any hurt, harm or danger. Look at the way that God gave Samson the motivation to defeat the Philistines (Judges 15:14-16). Look at the way that God gave David the motivation to defeat Goliath (1 Samuel 17). God will help you pass any test. He will help you triumph over anything, and that's why I say He is the generator of motivation.

THE REAL DEAL

Please let me have your attention. I just have to tell you who the real deal is. The real deal is the Almighty God. He is a mighty force that doesn't leave evil standing. He doesn't play any games. When God tells you to do something, do it because He doesn't like slow movers. The more you obey God, the more blessings you are going to receive. He is the God that gives you hope. He is the God that makes your dreams come true. God causes the sun and the stars to shine. He causes your car to keep moving when you are about to run out of gas. When a storm approaches, He causes it to pass over your home. God can do everything. All you have to do is believe in Him. He drives away evil like a hurricane rushes through a city. God is the One who blesses you to be healthy. He is the One who helps you move around. Take heed to what I'm saying because God is the real deal, the Creator of Evander Holyfield.

THE TRUE VISIONARY

Who is the true visionary? The Almighty God is the true visionary. He sees and knows what's going to happen in the future. God knows what you are going to do before you do it. He knows what you are going to say before you say it. That's why you have to be careful of what you do or say. God has a vision for all of us. His vision is a great vision. God has the best things waiting for us. We have to seek after His kingdom in order to receive those things.

God has high hopes for all of us. He has a place for each of us in His kingdom. Those who serve the Lord, continue to serve Him. He is going to bless you. To all the other people, turn aside from those false gods that you serve, and get to know the true Almighty God. He has so many blessings in store for you. *Trust in the Lord with all thine heart; and lean not unto thine own understanding* (Proverbs 3:5). Once you do that, watch how God shows you His vision, for He is the true visionary who sees everything.

THE WORD OF GOD

God knows that it's hard living in a world of sin. That's why He gave us His holy Word to guide us. It's up to you to believe it or not. But let me tell you this, my brothers and sisters; you will regret it if you don't believe in the Word of God because it is truly a weapon. My brothers and sisters, as you live, apply the Word of God to your life because living without Jesus Christ is no joke. We are created in His image and so let us stop playing games and live like Him and for Him. Again, people, don't play games because you will get caught in your own game and believe me, it's hard to get out. You can be on your way to hell if you continue to play games. There is no in between.

Allow me to testify, my brothers and sisters. There was a time in my life that I took my focus off God and focused on fleshly things. I prayed that God would have mercy on my soul, but if He didn't I wouldn't have blamed Him because I got selfish in my ways. My brothers and sisters, I prayed that the Lord would give me another chance in life and promised that I would not fail Him. Through the power of prayer and trusting in God's promises in His Word, God forgave me. You must believe in the Word of God. You must dwell on God's promises, fight for what you believe, and stop getting caught up! At this time, I thank God for His Word. I thank Him for both changing and teaching me how to forsake myself and focus fully on Him. I thank Him for His wonderful blessings and love. My friends, remember that life is not a game. It is up to you to believe God's Word so that you can discover your destiny and go for it. May the peace of God be in your minds and hearts. Stay focused on God and don't take Him for granted, for He is real. Remember that the Word of God is the key.

THERE IS A GOD

I know that things get hard for you at times. I know that sometimes, things get bad for you; but don't worry because there is a God. This God I'm talking about is not a small God He is a huge God. He is there with you during your good times and bad times. He lives inside of you. He is with you as you are reading this note of encouragement.

Whatever you do, don't stop reading the Bible. The Bible is your guide to life and through life. The Bible guides you to life, which is Jesus Christ. The Bible guides you through life on earth. It also tells you about more life, which is living eternally with God. Understand this, my brothers and sisters; the Bible is good for you. Don't be afraid to open it. Don't be afraid to believe in God. As you read the Bible, you will hear God's voice. God will speak to you. He will guide you through each situation that you face. He will make your life easier for you. God will tell you who to hang around and who not to hang around. God is all about your safety and well being. He will open doors for you that no man can open. All God is asking you to do is seek after His kingdom.

Now, don't get me wrong. Seeking after His kingdom is not easy because there is a coward out there trying to destroy you and his name is Satan, the fallen angel. God doesn't want you to fear him for He gave you the power to defeat him (Luke 10:19). Live your life with God. He will reveal His Son, Jesus Christ, and the Holy Spirit to you. There is a God, my brothers and sisters. Believe it!

YOU ARE NOTHING WITHOUT GOD

My dear brothers and sisters, I just want to remind you that you are nothing without God Almighty. God Almighty is the One who created you (Genesis 1:26-27). God Almighty created you in His image. God Almighty is the reason for your existence. Many people walk around this earth like they are God. They think that just because they are rich, they are better than everyone else. That money they are flaunting, God created it. That car they are driving, God made it.

What gives anyone the right to turn their nose up at other people? We are nothing without God. It is He who put the breath in our bodies. God blessed us to have a good reputation. How would any of us feel if God allowed all that to be taken away from us? Because of pride, many people forget the One who helped them reach the top.

If you are guilty of this, ask God for His forgiveness. Thank Him for finding you. Thank Him for understanding you when nobody else could. Last, but not least, tell God that you are nothing without Him and by acknowledging that, watch how the Great and Almighty God gives the increase to every area of your life. Why? Because you just came back to your senses and realized that God is the Truth.

YOU ARE SOMEBODY

Just to remind you, my wonderful saints and friends, God shows up whenever He decides to. When He shows up, it is amazing. He is awesome in everything He does. And so, my friends, don't put God on a shelf for anything. When someone tries to bring you down, just know you are somebody. You are somebody because God is your Father. Don't let anyone walk all over you. Don't let anyone control your life. To the women, you are queens, and to the men, you are kings. And we all know who the Ultimate King is; He is the Almighty God.

My friends, *Ye are the light of the world* (Matthew 5:14). Don't let anyone put out your light. Pray for those who are jealous of you. Continue to love God, and watch how many moves He makes on your behalf. Keep your head up and walk toward the Holy King. Just know as you walk toward the Him, there's going to be interference, but keep moving on because the Lord is a strong tower. *Let your light so shine before men, that they may see your good works, and glorify your Father which is in heaven* (Matthew 5:16). And on that note, my spiritual friends, remember you are all somebody.

YOU CAN'T LIVE TWO WAYS

Open up your mind to this encouragement that you are about to read. It is important that you take it in. There is only one God and He dwells in heaven. You have to serve Him at your own will; and remember, you can't live two ways. You can't serve God and Satan at the same time. You have to love one and hate the other, or despise one and serve the other (Matthew 6:24). I want all mankind to serve God, and hate Satan. I want everyone to love God, and despise Satan. You can't go to the strip club, and the next day, attend church. Going to the strip club is not serving God. You can't preach the Word of God, and have curse words coming out of your mouth the minute you stop talking about God. The Almighty God's words are pure, not filthy. Anyone who thinks that they are going to make it to the kingdom of heaven by serving both God and Satan, are fooling themselves.

God is in heaven. Satan is not. Be careful of the music you listen to. You can't listen to gospel, and the next minute, listen to illicit gangster rap or vulgar destructive music. That is being unequally yoked. There is only one way to make it to God, and that is through Jesus Christ. Jesus didn't live two ways. Jesus didn't serve two masters, He served one, and that was the Almighty God, so get your life together and know that you can't live two ways.

YOU CAN'T OUT POWER GOD

How are you doing, my brothers and sisters? God is a righteous force. One thing you can't do is out power Him. How are you going to out power a force that created you? He knows everything about you. God knows your next move in life. You can't figure God out, but He can figure you out. He is smooth in everything He does. The heavens praise Him, and hell fear Him. I'm talking about the God who shakes the whole world when He speaks. I'm talking about the God who makes demons tremble. He doesn't play any games. God is a smooth operator. Remember the way that He eased His way on in the fiery furnace to protect the Hebrew boys (Daniel 3:25). I mean, He is awesome. He out powers everything and everybody. He is the Lord of Host. I love Him and will do anything for Him.

God, You are a mighty force. We know that You have all the power to conquer over our enemies. You are our Father, and we know that nothing can out power You, for You are the Creator of power.

YOU CAN'T USE GOD

What's up, my brothers and sisters? What's going on? God is a trustworthy God. When you need Him, He is always there. He is there even when you think He's not. You are not the only person in the world. Just like you need help from God, other people also need His help. I'm just here to remind you that you can't use God. Many people try to use God to get what they want. They say they love God, but don't really mean it. In church, they put on an act as if they are praising God.

Wherefore the Lord said, Forasmuch as this people draw near me with their mouth, and with their lips do honor me, but have removed their heart far from me, and their fear toward me is taught by the precept of men (Isaiah 29:13). Do these people think God is stupid? God knows everyone's intentions. He knows if we are doing things from our hearts, or doing things to uplift ourselves. God knows what we are going to do before we do it. Instead of trying to use God, we should have faith and believe in Him. God always keeps His promises. Does man think God is not going to bless him? What do we take God as? He owns everything. He is the richest force in the universe. He is not selfish like many of us. Everything He does is for the good.

And it shall come to pass, if thou shalt hearken diligently unto the voice of the Lord thy God, to observe and to do all his commandments which I command thee this day, that the Lord thy God will set thee on high above all nations of the earth (Deuteronomy 28:1). Hearken unto the Lord's commandments and remember that you can't use Him.

YOU DON'T GIVE GOD ORDERS

First of all, who does mankind think he is to try to give God orders or try to tell Him what to do? God is not our servant, we are His servants. He called us to serve Him, and not Him to serve us. If one person doesn't want to serve God, fine. God has plenty of other people who desire to serve Him. Those that choose not to serve Him are the ones who will be missing out on the riches of God. Do they think God is going to cry if they stop serving Him? God is full of joy and happiness. Surely, God loves each of us and surely God cares for us all, but He's not going to stop living if we stop serving Him. God doesn't need to be delivered. God doesn't need to be healed. God doesn't need Jesus Christ to make it to heaven. We need those wonderful things. We need Jesus Christ. We need deliverance. We need healing. Many people ask God to work things out for them, and help them, and they ask God to bless them, but no one is authorized to tell Him what to do or give Him orders. He is the One who is sitting on the throne of heaven. He is the One who has wonderful and majestic angels worshiping Him. He is the One who appointed all of us to serve Him. So what we need to do is relax, serve God with joy, and get ready to receive our inheritance when we depart from this wonderful place.

YOU JUST DON'T KNOW

Everyday, you should give thanks to God, for He blesses you to see another rising of the sun. He is the most loving Spirit in the universe. You just don't know how special you are to God. He talks about you all the time. God tells His holy heavenly angels how faithful you are. He also tells His Son, who sits on the righthand side of the throne, how unique you are. You just don't know that God has already prepared a place for you, and it is so tremendous. God loves you in a special way. He loves you more than you love yourself. You just don't know how precious you are to God. Everyday, He shields and protects you from your enemies. He comforts you on a daily basis. Tell God how much you love Him. He loves to hear it. Shower God with love. Spread His name with joyfulness. Our Father is so gentle. Even when we act like fools, He nourishes us because He knows how we are. He knew how we were before He placed us on this planet. You just don't know that God is a true Provider so continue to stay focused on Him because He is a great Father.

Chapter Three

ENCOURAGING

A GOD YOU SHOULD TRUST

A God you should trust is all about righteousness
A God you should trust is all about peace
A God you should trust is all about holiness
A God you should trust is all about happiness
A God you should trust is all about salvation
A God you should trust is all about love
A God you should trust is all about kindness
A God you should trust is all about eternal life
That God you should trust is the Almighty God

A GUARANTEE

It's a guarantee that God will bless you
It's a guarantee that God will heal you
It's a guarantee that God will save you
It's a guarantee that God will deliver you
It's a guarantee that God will mold you
It's a guarantee that God will hold you
It's a guarantee that God will preserve you
It's a guarantee that God will love you

A MAGNIFICENT BLESSING

A magnificent blessing is being born again
A magnificent blessing is having joy
A magnificent blessing is having peace
A magnificent blessing is having love
A magnificent blessing is having patience
A magnificent blessing is having forgiveness
A magnificent blessing is having confidence
A magnificent blessing is having the Holy Spirit
A magnificent blessing is having eternal life in heavenly paradise

ALL I NEED

All I need is more peace
All I need is everlasting joy
All I need is more understanding
All I need is more wisdom
All I need is more knowledge
All I need is love
All I need is more cleansing
All I need is Jesus Christ
All I need is God

ALWAYS REMEMBER

Always remember that God loves you
Always remember that Jesus Christ loves you
Always remember that the Holy Spirit loves you
Always remember that God's Holy Angels love you
Always remember that Abraham loves you
Always remember that Moses loves you
Always remember that Paul the apostle loves you
Always remember that I love you

ARE YOU WILLING?

Are you willing to praise God?
Are you willing to worship God?
Are you willing to bless God?
Are you willing to thank God?
Are you willing to follow God?
Are you willing to obey God?
Are you willing to trust God?
Are you willing to hear God?
Are you willing to die for God?
Are you willing to love God?

BE AT PEACE

Be at peace with God
Be at peace with Jesus Christ
Be at peace with the Holy Spirit
Be at peace with your mother
Be at peace with your father
Be at peace with your sister
Be at peace with your brother
Be at peace with your husband
Be at peace with your wife
Be at peace with your children
Be at peace with yourself

BE DETERMINED

Be determined to serve God
Be determined to bless God
Be determined to worship God
Be determined to honor God
Be determined to obey God
Be determined to follow God
Be determined to live for God
Be determined to seek God

BE HAPPY

Be happy to obey God
Be happy to bless God
Be happy to praise God
Be happy to serve God
Be happy to trust God
Be happy to have faith in God
Be happy to dwell with God
Be happy to love God

BE QUIET

Be quiet and listen to God
Be quiet and listen to Jesus Christ
Be quiet and listen to Holy Spirit
Be quiet and listen to the holy angels
Be quiet and listen to your parents
Be quiet and listen to your teachers
Be quiet and listen to your elders
Be quiet and listen because you don't know everything

BE READY

Be ready to obey God
Be ready to face the enemy
Be ready to fight the good fight of faith
Be ready to go to war
Be ready to honor the Lord
Be ready to face the Lord
Be ready to feel pain
Be ready to endure pain
Be ready to bless the Lord
Be ready to gain peace

BE WILLING

Be willing to praise God
Be willing to bless God
Be willing to serve God
Be willing to honor God
Be willing to obey God
Be willing to acknowledge God
Be willing to depend on God
Be willing to love God

BEFORE YOU ENTER THE SANCTUARY

Put away negative things
Put away bad reports
Forgive those who wrongfully use you
Greet your brothers and sisters
Have joyful praises in your mind and heart
Have the Holy Trinity in your mind and heart
Have the return of Christ in your mind and heart
Be ready to praise God
Be ready to honor the Holy Trinity
Be ready to honor your ministers
MAY GOD BLESS YOU AND I LOVE YOU

BELIEVE

Believe in the Lord, for He will help you
Believe in the Lord's Word
Believe in the Lord with faith
Believe in the Lord with confidence
Believe in the Lord with strength
Believe in the Lord with your whole heart
Believe in the Lord with your mind
Believe in the Lord, for your soul belongs to Him
Believe in the Lord, for He is righteous
Believe in the Lord, for He is a great King
Believe in the Lord, for He can bless you
Believe in the Lord, for He will heal you
Believe in the Lord, for He will anoint you
Believe in the Lord with praises
Believe in the Lord, for He has prepared a place for you

BLESSED

Blessed are they who believe in God
Blessed are they who have faith in God
Blessed are they who trust in God
Blessed are they who rely on God
Blessed are they who rejoice in God
Blessed are they who turn from their wicked ways
Blessed are they who accept Jesus Christ
Blessed are they who are bought with a price

BRING HAPPINESS

Bring happiness in your home
Bring happiness on your job
Bring happiness on yourself
Bring happiness on your friends
Bring happiness to the church
Bring happiness to your school
Bring happiness to your family
Bring happiness everywhere you go
Bring happiness, for God is in you and He loves you

BY THE GRACE

By the grace of God, you have life
By the grace of God, you are saved
By the grace of God, you are blessed
By the grace of God, you are healed
By the grace of God, you are delivered
By the grace of God, you are free
By the grace of God, you are unique
By the grace of God, you have eternal life

CHANGE

God, change my mind into pure thoughts
God, change my soul to Your awesome power
God, change my heart to a Christ-like heart
God, change my ways to godly ways
God, change my life so I can make it to the top
God, change my body so I can dwell with You
God, change everything about me so I can preach about You
God, change my entire life so I can be a body of Christ
God, change me so I can have eternal life

CHECK HIM OUT

God is great; check Him out
Jesus Christ is intelligent; check Him out
God is smooth; check Him out
Jesus Christ is marvelous; check Him out
God is perfect; check Him out
Jesus Christ is amazing; check Him out
God is wonderful; check Him out
Jesus Christ is a Comforter; check Him out
God is mighty; check Him out
Jesus Christ is real; check Him out
God is the Holy King; check Him out

CLAP YOUR HANDS

Clap your hands to praise God
Clap your hands to glorify God
Clap your hands to honor God
Clap your hands to serve God
Clap your hands to uplift God
Clap your hands to please God
Clap your hands to respect God
Clap your hands to obey God
Clap your hands to proclaim God
Clap your hands to magnify God

CONTINUE

Continue to bless God
Continue to serve God
Continue to praise God
Continue to worship God
Continue to obey God
Continue to honor God
Continue to seek after God
Continue to respect God
Continue to adore God
Continue to love God

CONTROL

God, control my mind
God, control my heart
God, control my soul
God, control my life
God, control my church
God, control my family
God, control my enemies
God, control my country
God, control this world
God, control everything

COUNT IT ALL JOY

Count it all joy, for you are a servant of God
Count it all joy, for Jesus Christ dwells in you
Count it all joy, for Jesus loves you
Count it all joy, for Jesus is your peace
Count it all joy, for in God, there is victory
Count it all joy, for God is there for you
Count it all joy, for God has prepared a place for you
Count it all joy, for God smiles upon you

DEPEND ON GOD

Depend on God because He will guide you
Depend on God because He will strengthen you
Depend on God because He loves you
Depend on God because He will never forsake you
Depend on God because He will never leave you alone
Depend on God because He will protect you
Depend on God because He will help you
Depend on God because He will bless you
Depend on God because He is mighty
Depend on God because He never fails

DO YOU?

Do you believe in God?
Do you trust God?
Do you have faith in God?
Do you respect God?
Do you obey God?
Do you honor God?
Do you glorify God?
Do you praise God?
Do you fear God?
Do you love God?
Do you desire to dwell with God?

DON'T

Do not serve God just to get blessed
Do not serve God just to be seen
Do not serve God just to get material things
Do not serve God just to get rich
Do not serve God just to be popular
Do not serve God just to be successful
Do not serve God just to be spectacular
But serve God just because He loves you and you love Him

DON'T BE MOVED

Don't be moved by the games that Satan plays
Don't be moved by fear
Don't be moved, for God is on your side
Don't be moved, for you are strong
Don't be moved, for Jesus has the victory
Don't be moved, for God has all the power
Don't be moved so God can use you
Don't be moved, for God is for you

DON'T HATE

Don't hate because God is blessing someone
Don't hate because God is elevating someone
Don't hate because God is anointing someone
Don't hate because God is preserving someone
Don't hate because God is transforming someone
Don't hate because God is delivering someone
Don't hate because God is helping someone
Don't hate because it's not necessary

DON'T HESITATE

Don't hesitate when it comes to blessing God
Don't hesitate when it comes to worshipping God
Don't hesitate when it comes to acknowledging God
Don't hesitate when it comes to preaching about God
Don't hesitate when it comes to meditating on God
Don't hesitate when it comes to praising God
Don't hesitate when it comes to obeying God

DON'T LET GO

Don't let go of God's wisdom
Don't let go of God's knowledge
Don't let go of God's understanding
Don't let go of your confidence
Don't let go of your faith
Don't let go of your joy
Don't let go of your peace
Don't let go of your family
Don't let go of your trust in God
Don't let go of your patience
Don't let go of your wit
Don't let go of your integrity
Don't let go of your love
Don't let go of God's commandments
Don't let go of Jesus Christ
Don't let go of the Almighty God

DON'T TAKE

Don't take your family for granted
Don't take yourself for granted
Don't take people's kindness for granted
Don't take your boss for granted
Don't take your teacher for granted
Don't take your ministers for granted
Don't take the Holy Lamb, Jesus Christ, for granted
Don't take the greatest Father, the Almighty God, for granted

ENJOY

Enjoy the gifts that God grants you
Enjoy the blessings that God gives to you
Enjoy the love that God gives to you
Enjoy the magnificent earth that God created
Enjoy the wonderful family that God blessed you with
Enjoy the wonderful church that you attend
Enjoy yourself, because you are royalty
Enjoy the Holy Spirit, which is your Comforter (John 14:26)
Enjoy the Holy Lamb, which is the majestic Jesus Christ
Enjoy Yahweh, which is the peaceful Almighty God
Enjoy the New Jerusalem, for you will be there forever

FATHER GOD

Father God, let Your Spirit pour upon us
Father God, let Your love shine upon us
Father God, let Your blessings rain down upon us
Father God, let Your power come down upon us
Father God, let Your faith come down upon us
Father God, let Your might come down upon us
Father God, let Your glory come down upon us
Father God, let Your kingdom come down upon us
Father God, please just let us dwell with You

FEAR NOTHING

It is good to have a God that will take all of your fears away. I love God, for He has taken all of my fears away.

Fear nothing, because the Lord is on your side
Fear nothing, because the Lord gave you power to rebuke Satan
Fear nothing, because you are a soldier of the Lord
Fear nothing, because you do have courage
Fear nothing, because God loves you
Fear nothing, because you are somebody
Fear nothing, because you are saved
Fear nothing, because God is in you
Fear nothing, because you are blessed
Fear nothing, because you are important
Fear nothing, because God is your rod and staff
Fear nothing, because you are more than a conqueror
(Romans 8:37)

FEEL

Feel the Holy Spirit moving in you
Feel the Holy Spirit healing you
Feel the Holy Spirit loving you
Feel the Holy Spirit relaxing you
Feel the Holy Spirit guiding you
Feel the Holy Spirit burning in you
Feel the Holy Spirit convicting you
Feel the Holy Spirit nourishing you

FEEL ME

Feel me when I say God is good
Feel me when I say Jesus is real
Feel me when I say God is awesome
Feel me when I say Jesus is Lord
Feel me when I say God is perfect
Feel me when I say Jesus is love
Feel me when I say God is peace
Feel me when I say Jesus is wonderful
Feel me when I say God is a great Father
Feel me when I say Jesus is amazing
Feel me when I say God is everlasting

FOCUS

Focus on God
Focus on Jesus Christ
Focus on the Holy Spirit
Focus on your brothers and sisters in Christ Jesus
Focus on the souls you are going to touch
Focus on the people you are going to help save
Focus on pleasing God
Focus on living eternally

FORGIVE ME

Forgive me, God, for being selfish
Forgive me, God, for being inconsiderate
Forgive me, God, for being impatient
Forgive me, God, for being doubtful
Forgive me, God, for being ungrateful
Forgive me, God, for being disobedient
Forgive me, God, for being negative
Forgive me, God, for being lustful
Forgive me God for being fearful
Forgive me, God, for being childish
Forgive me, God, for being a hypocrite
Forgive me, God, for being a liar
Forgive me, God, for being ignorant
Forgive me, God, for being jealous
Forgive me, God, for idolizing
Forgive me, God, for committing adultery
Forgive me, God, for breaking covenants
Forgive me, God, for blasphemy
Forgive me, God, for playing games

GIVE GOD THE CREDIT

Give God the credit for creating you
Give God the credit for preserving you
Give God the credit for protecting you
Give God the credit for sheltering you
Give God the credit for blessing you
Give God the credit for healing you
Give God the credit for guiding you
Give God the credit for choosing you
Give God the credit for trusting you
Give God the credit for forgiving you

GIVE US THE STRENGTH

God, give us the strength to survive
God, give us the strength to praise You
God, give us the strength to press
God, give us the strength to bring You souls
God, give us the strength to shake things off of us
God, give us the strength to continue to love
God, give us the strength to endure pain
God, give us the strength to serve You
God, give us the strength to be free

GLORY TO GOD

Glory to God, for creating the earth
Glory to God, for creating heaven
Glory to God, for creating the solar system
Glory to God, for creating man
Glory to God, for being majestic
Glory to God, for sending His Son on earth
Glory to God, for He is mighty
Glory to God, for being in our lives
Glory to God, for His wonderful nature
Glory to God, for not giving up on us
Glory to God, for His mercy endureth forever (Psalm 118:1)
Glory to God, for watching over us
Glory to God, for He is powerful
Glory to God, for He is a true hero
Glory to God, for His love lasts eternally

GO TO GOD

Go to God for comfort
Go to God for peace
Go to God for motivation
Go to God for love
Go to God for understanding
Go to God for knowledge
Go to God for joy
Go to God for life
Go to God for protection
Go to God for direction
Go to God for forgiveness
Go to God for power
Go to God for compassion

GOD DOESN'T MIND

God does not mind you praising Him
God does not mind you blessing Him
God does not mind you worshiping Him
God does not mind you obeying Him
God does not mind you following Him
God does not mind you hearkening to Him
God does not mind you honoring Him
God does not mind you loving Him
For those things are what He loves and created you to do

GOD HAS THE RIGHT

God has the right to discipline you
God has the right to rebuke you
God has the right to bless you
God has the right to protect you
God has the right to judge you
God has the right to love you
God has the right to do anything that He pleases to do

GOD IS

God is the mightiest force in the universe. He is the strongest wind that blows. God is the most beautiful flower in the field. He is the tree that stands the tallest in the jungle. God is the largest wave in the ocean. He is the brightest light that shines in the sky. God is the Commander in Chief of the holy army. He is the missile that is going to destroy the evil military. God is the softest cloud in the sky. He is the sweetest honey in the beehive. God is that mailman who always delivers on time. He is the foundation that keeps your house standing. God is the purest water there is to drink. He is the strong nail that holds your pictures in place on the walls. God is the most genuine leather there is to wear. He is the thread that never runs out. Above all these things, God is your Heavenly Father and best Friend.

GOD IS II

God is perfection
God is gentle
God is mighty
God is trustworthy
God is #1
God is awesome
God is exciting
God is loving
God is the best
God is the King who rules over all

GOD IS CAPABLE

Good morning, my friends. It's a lovely day that the Almighty God has blessed us to see. I just want to tell you that God loves you, and that He's capable of doing anything.

God is capable of blessing you with peace
God is capable of blessing you to teach
God is capable of helping you soar
God is capable of making you roar
God is capable of making you shine
God is capable of making you fine
God is capable of making you rich
God is capable of keeping you from becoming sick
God is capable of making you bold
God is capable of blessing you with fine riches and gold

GOD IS IN

God is in my mind
God is in my heart
God is in my life
God is in my ears
God is in my sights
God is in my voice
God is in my walk
God is in my church
God is in my family
God is in my future

GOD

God, bless me to be a force in You
God, bless me to be more spiritual in You
God, bless me to be strong in You
God, bless me to be honest in You
God, bless me to be a minister for You
God, bless me to be bold in You
God, bless me to be gentle in You
God, bless me to dwell with You

GOD IS NOT

God is not a joke
God is not a toy
God is not a game
God is not your enemy
God is not a monster
God is not a hypocrite
God is not a liar
God is not an abuser
God is not an accuser
God is not a loser

GOD IS NOT II

God is not begging you to praise Him
God is not forcing you to serve Him
God is not begging you to worship Him
God is not forcing you to follow Him
God is not begging you to bless Him
God is not forcing you to honor Him
God is not begging you to please Him
God is not forcing you to obey Him
God is not begging you to sacrifice unto Him
God is not forcing you to love Him

GOD IS THE GREATEST

God is the greatest Father
God is the greatest Mother
God is the greatest Brother
God is the greatest Sister
God is the greatest Preacher
God is the greatest Teacher
God is the greatest Force
God is the greatest Source
God is the greatest Pastor
God is the greatest Master
God is the greatest Spirit

GOD IS WORTHY II

God is worthy to be praised
God is worthy to be blessed
God is worthy to be glorified
God is worthy to be magnified
God is worthy to be honored
God is worthy to be uplifted
God is worthy to be served
God is worthy to be obeyed
God is worthy to be King
God is worthy to be loved forever

GOD KNOWS

God knows that you are not perfect
God knows that you need Him
God knows that you desire to be successful
God knows that you desire to get married
God knows that you love Him
God knows that you are sorry for what you have done in the past
God knows that you have sinned
God knows that you are hurt and have been hurt
God knows that you are hungry for righteousness
God knows your every need and everything about you

GOOD MORNING

Good morning to You, God
Good morning to You, Jesus Christ
Good morning to You, Holy Spirit
Good morning to you, four living creatures who surround the throne of God
Good morning to you, 24 elders who worship our God in spirit and in truth
Good morning to all of you, heavenly host
Good morning to all of you, children of God

HAVE FAITH

Have faith in God, for He is powerful
Have faith in God, for He is righteous
Have faith in God, for He is holy
Have faith in God, for He is perfect
Have faith in God, for He is just
Have faith in God, for He is protection
Have faith in God, for He is salvation
Have faith in God, for He is mighty
Have faith in God, for He is a great Father
Have faith in God, for He is love

HEAR ME

Hear me, God, when I say I love You
Hear me, God, when I say I fear You
Hear me, God, when I say I respect You
Hear me, God, when I say I adore You
Hear me, God, when I say I want Your riches
Hear me, God, when I say You are mighty
Hear me, God, when I say forgive me
Hear me, God, when I say I'm sorry
Hear me, God, when I say I want to dwell with You
Hear me, God, when I say may peace be with You

HEAR

Hear the Word of God
Hear the true ministers of God
Hear the true prophets of God
Hear the true missionaries of God
Hear the true evangelists of God
Hear the true bishops of God
Hear the true preachers of God
Hear the true people of God
Hear the amazing and awesome Son of God

HEAVEN

Heaven is a place filled with glory
Heaven is a place filled with love
Heaven is a place filled with joy
Heaven is a place filled with peace
Heaven is a place filled with angels
Heaven is a place filled with blessings
Heaven is a place filled with God's brightness
Heaven is a place that never gets dark
Heaven is a place where my Lord and Savior dwells
Heaven is a place where my Heavenly Father dwells

HOLD ON

It feels so good to be a Christian. Even though we go through hard times, through it all, we know we are going to be victorious. My friends, just hold on because at the end of your trials and tribulations, you are going to receive a great reward.

Hold on to your faith
Hold on to your patience
Hold on to your love
Hold on to your strength
Hold on to your goals
Hold on to God's promises
Hold on to your might
Hold on to your hopes
Hold on to the armor of God
Hold on to the Word of God
Hold on to your good character
Hold on to your heart
Hold on to your dreams
Hold on to your virtue
Hold on to Jesus Christ
Hold on to God
Hold on so you can live eternally

I AM DESIGNED

I am designed to bless God
I am designed to praise God
I am designed to worship God
I am designed to follow God
I am designed to obey God
I am designed to honor God
I am designed to adore God
I am designed to love God

I CAN'T STOP

I can't stop praising God
I can't stop blessing God
I can't stop talking about God
I can't stop preaching about God
I can't stop honoring God
I can't stop shouting for God
I can't stop reading about God
I can't stop teaching about God
I can't stop speaking to God
I can't stop loving God

I CHALLENGE

I challenge you to praise God
I challenge you to bless God
I challenge you to worship God
I challenge you to serve God
I challenge you to honor God
I challenge you to obey God
I challenge you to abide with God
I challenge you to depend on God
I challenge you to believe in God
I challenge you to stand tall in God

I HUNGER

I hunger for God's Word
I hunger for God's blessings
I hunger for God's righteousness
I hunger for God's grace
I hunger for God's presence
I hunger for God's peace
I hunger for God's power
I hunger for God's anointing
I hunger for Jesus Christ

I LIVE

I live to praise God
I live to honor God
I live to worship God
I live to bless God
I live to obey God
I live to follow God
I live to love God
I live for God

I PROMISED

I promised God that I will serve Him
I promised God that I will bless Him
I promised God that I will praise Him
I promised God that I will glorify Him
I promised God that I will obey Him
I promised God that I will acknowledge Him
I promised God that I will seek after Him
I promised God that I will trust Him
I promised God that I will hearken to Him
I promised God that I will worship Him for all eternity

I REFUSE

I refuse to be selfish with God
I refuse to be selfish with Jesus Christ
I refuse to be selfish with the Holy Spirit
I refuse to be selfish with my mother
I refuse to be selfish with my brother
I refuse to be selfish with my sister
I refuse to be selfish with my spouse
I refuse to be selfish with my neighbor
I refuse to be selfish with myself

I'M PRAYING

I'm praying that God continues to strengthen us
I'm praying that God continues to move us
I'm praying that God continues to discipline us
I'm praying that God continues to bless us
I'm praying that God continues to uplift us
I'm praying that God continues to excite us
I'm praying that God continues to shake us
I'm praying that God continues to break us
I'm praying that God continues to mold us
I'm praying that God continues to hold us
I'm praying that God continues to equip us so we can be a strong body of Christ

IN THE PALM OF GOD'S HAND

In the palm of God's hand, there is love
In the palm of God's hand, there is safety
In the palm of God's hand, there is protection
In the palm of God's hand, there is security
In the palm of God's hand, there is power
In the palm of God's hand, there is comfort
In the palm of God's hand, there is healing
In the palm of God's hand, there is deliverance
In the palm of God's hand, there is peace
In the palm of God's hand, there is joy
In the palm of God's hand, there is Jesus Christ
In the palm of God's hand, there is the Holy Spirit
In the palm of God's hand, there is eternal life

IT FEELS GOOD

It feels good to bless God
It feels good to love God
It feels good to be blessed by God
It feels good to be anointed by God
It feels good to be renewed by God
It feels good to be uplifted by God
It feels good to be loved by God
It feels good to be sheltered by God
It feels good to be comforted by God

IT IS A BLESSING

It is a blessing to be healed by God
It is a blessing to be honored by God
It is a blessing to be loved by God
It is a blessing to be delivered by God
It is a blessing to be spoken of by God
It is a blessing to be blessed by God
It is a blessing to walk with God
It is a blessing to be nurtured by God
It is a blessing to serve God
It is a blessing to live with God

IT IS GOD'S WORD

It is God's Word that keeps me living
It is God's Word that keeps me standing
It is God's Word that keeps me going
It is God's Word that teaches me to forgive
It is God's Word that teaches me to pray
It is God's Word that teaches me to obey

IT IS TRUE!

It is true that God is faithful!
It is true that Jesus Christ is remarkable!
It is true that God is mighty!
It is true that Jesus Christ is sensational!
It is true that God is the Holy King!
It is true that Jesus Christ is loving!
It is true that God is powerful!
It is true that Jesus Christ is forgiving!
It is true that Jesus Christ is on His way back!
It is true that God loves you!

IT WAS GOD

It was God who created you
It was God who blessed you
It was God who shielded you
It was God who preserved you
It was God who comforted you
It was God who sheltered you
It was God who healed you
It was God who anointed you
It was God who lifted you
It was God who chose you

IT'S A WONDERFUL FEELING

Feel me on this piece that you are reading. It's a wonderful feeling to be a servant or child of God. The One who is capable of doing all things is the Almighty God. All we have to do is obey Him. God is the One who brings you out of tough situations. He is the One that uplifts your spirit. Talk to God. He loves a good conversation.

It's a wonderful feeling when God speaks to you
It's a wonderful feeling when God touches you
It's a wonderful feeling when God elevates you
It's a wonderful feeling when God restores you
It's a wonderful feeling when God heals you
It's a wonderful feeling when God comforts you
It's a wonderful feeling when God blesses you
It's a wonderful feeling when God approves of you
It's a wonderful feeling when God motivates you
It's a wonderful feeling when you know that God loves you

IT'S MY NATURE

It's my nature to love God
It's my nature to love Jesus Christ
It's my nature to obey God
It's my nature to trust God
It's my nature to have faith in God
It's my nature to honor God
It's my nature to follow Jesus Christ
It's my nature to praise God
It's my nature to worship God
It's my nature to walk with and adore God

IT'S NOT A COMPETITION

It's not a competition when it comes to worshiping God
It's not a competition when it comes to serving God
It's not a competition when it comes to honoring God
It's not a competition when it comes to obeying God
It's not a competition when it comes to acknowledging God
It's not a competition when it comes to loving God
It's not a competition when it comes to praising God
It's not a competition when it comes to blessing God

IT'S NOT

It's not money that blesses you
It's not cars that bless you
It's not houses that bless you
It's not your wife who blesses you
It's not your husband who blesses you
It's not your brother who blesses you
It's not your sister who blesses you
It's not material things that bless you
It's the true and living God Almighty who blesses you

IT'S NOT WORTH IT

It's not worth it, being depressed
It's not worth it, being sad
It's not worth it, being hateful
It's not worth it, being selfish
It's not worth it, being jealous
It's not worth it, being deceitful
It's not worth it, being worried
It's not worth it, using bad language
It's not worth it, being a criminal
It's not worth it, serving Satan

IT'S YOUR CALLING

It's your calling to praise God
It's your calling to serve Jesus Christ
It's your calling to adore the Holy Spirit
It's your calling to worship God
It's your calling to honor Jesus Christ
It's your calling to appreciate the Holy Spirit
It's your calling to obey God
It's your calling to follow Jesus Christ
It's your calling to love the Holy Spirit
It's your calling to respect the Holy Trinity

KEEP ON

I thank God for the people who encourage and motivate others. They are showing God that they are not selfish. They spend their precious and valuable time caring, loving, and doing for others. I just want to tell them to keep on...

Keep on loving others
Keep on motivating others
Keep on caring for others
Keep on sharing with others
Keep on giving to others
Keep on doing for others
Keep on encouraging others
Keep on teaching others
Keep on preaching to others
Keep on pushing others
Keep on leading others by a good example
Keep on comforting others

KEEP PRAYING

Keep praying for the children
Keep praying for the homeless
Keep praying for the poor
Keep praying for the drug dealers
Keep praying for the prostitutes
Keep praying for the rich
Keep praying for the preachers
Keep praying for the government
Keep praying for everyone's family
Keep praying for the church
Keep praying for the whole world
Keep praying for yourself

KEEP PRESSING

Keep pressing toward your goals
Keep pressing to get closer to God
Keep pressing to be successful
Keep pressing to be the best
Keep pressing to make an impact in this world
Keep pressing to set a good example
Keep pressing toward greatness
Keep pressing to graduate
Keep pressing to make your family proud
Keep pressing to make yourself proud
Keep pressing to make Jesus Christ proud
Keep pressing to glorify God

LET YOUR MIND DWELL

Let your mind dwell with God
Let your mind dwell with Jesus Christ
Let your mind dwell with heaven
Let your mind dwell with peace
Let your mind dwell with love
Let your mind dwell with caring
Let your mind dwell with unity
Let your mind dwell with pure thoughts
Let your mind dwell with humbleness
Let your mind dwell with eternal life

LISTEN

Listen to God
Listen to Jesus Christ
Listen to God's apostles
Listen to God's servants
Listen to God's angels
Listen to God's spiritual counselors
Listen to God's prophets
Listen to Jesus' disciples
Listen to God, for He is a great guidance counselor
Listen to God, for His mercy endures forever

LIVE

Live to please God
Live to worship God
Live to obey God
Live to serve God
Live to depend on God
Live to honor God
Live to trust in God
Live to have faith in God
Live to love God
Live to dwell with God

MAY PEACE BE WITH YOU

God knows it's hard living in this world. Sometimes you may feel that you are alone. This world has a lot of violence in it, but don't be one of those people that participate in it. May peace be with you.

May peace be with you in your home
May peace be with you on your job
May peace be with you in school
May peace be with you in your car
May peace be with you in your mind
May peace be with you in your heart
May peace be with you in your soul
May peace be with you in your conversation
May peace be with you in your actions
May peace be with you on the airplane
May peace be with you in God

MY GOAL

My goal is to bless God
My goal is to serve God
My goal is to walk with God
My goal is to follow God
My goal is to trust God
My goal is to believe in God
My goal is to continue to love God
My goal is to live with God forever

MY LIFE

My life is with God
My life is with Jesus Christ
My life is with the Holy Spirit
My life is with God's Holy Angels
My life is with the body of Christ
My life is eternal life

MY MIND

My mind is on God
My mind is on Jesus Christ
My mind is on the Holy Spirit
My mind is on peace
My mind is on joy
My mind is on love
My mind is on eternal life

NOTHING CAN STOP

Nothing can stop the force of God
Nothing can stop the love of God
Nothing can stop the power of God
Nothing can stop the words of God
Nothing can stop the ways of God
Nothing can stop the timing of God
Nothing can stop the Son of God
Nothing can stop the servants of God
Nothing can stop the glory of God
Nothing can stop the children of God

NOTHING CAN STOP II

Nothing can stop God from loving you
Nothing can stop God from blessing you
Nothing can stop God from shielding you
Nothing can stop God from protecting you
Nothing can stop God from helping you
Nothing can stop God from comforting you
Nothing can stop God from believing in you
Nothing can stop God from shining bright in you

PARTICIPATE

Participate in blessing God
Participate in serving God
Participate in praising God
Participate in worshiping God
Participate in uplifting God
Participate in preaching about God
Participate in praying to God
Participate in magnifying God
Participate in believing in God
Participate in loving God

PLEASE GOD II

Please God by doing good
Please God by helping others
Please God by encouraging others
Please God by blessing others
Please God by paying your tithes and offering
Please God by being obedient
Please God by praising Him
Please God by blessing Him
Please God by trusting in Him
Please God by loving Him
Please God by having faith in Him

PRAISE GOD

Praise God for His wonderful kindness
Praise God for His wonderful blessings
Praise God for His wonderful anointing
Praise God for His wonderful tender mercies
Praise God for His wonderful love
Praise God for His wonderful healings
Praise God for His wonderful peace
Praise God for His wonderful smile
Praise God for His wonderful creation
Praise God for His wonderful and remarkable Son

PROVE TO GOD

Prove to God how much you love Him
Prove to God how much you adore Him
Prove to God how much you trust Him
Prove to God how much you honor Him
Prove to God how much you have faith in Him
Prove to God how much you respect Him
Prove to God how much you want to be like Him
Prove to God how much you want to dwell with Him

    Abraham proved it by his willingness to sacrifice his son. David proved it by defeating Goliath. Moses proved it by departing the Red Sea. Shadrach, Meshach, and Abednego proved it by getting into the fiery furnace. Daniel proved it in the lion's den. Harriet Tubman proved it by helping free slaves. Rosa Parks proved it by not giving up her seat. Martin Luther King Jr. proved it by leading the marches of freedom. The greatest of them all, Jesus Christ, proved it by dying on a cross, freeing everyone from their sins.

PROVE TO YOUR ENEMIES

Prove to your enemies that you are not weak
Prove to your enemies that you are brave
Prove to your enemies that you are a soldier
Prove to your enemies that you are a child of God
Prove to your enemies that you are strong
Prove to your enemies that you are prestigious
Prove to your enemies that you are virtuous
Prove to your enemies that you are a warrior
Prove to your enemies that you are somebody
Prove to your enemies that you have everlasting joy
Prove to your enemies that you are more than a conqueror
Prove to your enemies that you can be successful
Prove to your enemies that Jesus Christ is your Savior
Prove to your enemies that God is your Heavenly Father
Prove to your enemies that you are going to live eternally
Prove to your enemies that God is love

REACH TOWARD HEAVEN

Reach toward heaven for your blessings
Reach toward heaven for your anointing
Reach toward heaven for your healing
Reach toward heaven for wisdom
Reach toward heaven for love
Reach toward heaven for joy
Reach toward heaven for peace
Reach toward heaven for knowledge
Reach toward heaven for understanding
Reach toward heaven for God

REBUKE

Many of us have to get over our fears and get closer to God. He gives us the power to rebuke.

Rebuke the bad things that come in your mind
Rebuke the people who doubt you
Rebuke the bad things that you use to do
Rebuke the people that abuse you
Rebuke the ones who accuse you
Rebuke the snakes that come upon you in your life
Rebuke the pit your enemies set up for you to fall in
Rebuke the teacher who didn't give you the grade that
 you deserved
Rebuke the people that tell you lies
Rebuke the ones that despise you
Rebuke the people who are ungrateful
Rebuke the people who are inconsiderate
Rebuke the people who are self-centered
Rebuke the ones who are hypocrites
Above all, rebuke Satan, because he is the master of them all.

REJOICE

Rejoice, for the Lord reigns
Rejoice, for the Lord is merciful
Rejoice, for the Lord is full of love
Rejoice, for the Lord is full of kindness
Rejoice, for the Lord is mighty
Rejoice, for the Lord is preparing a place for you
Rejoice, for the Lord loves you
Rejoice, for the Lord has His eyes on you

RELAX

Relax, you are going to get that car
Relax, you are going to get that house
Relax, you are going to get that wife
Relax, you are going to get that husband
Relax, you are going to be successful
Relax, you are going to be prosperous
Relax, you are going to have great children
Relax, you are going to be helpful to others
Relax, God is going to take care of you
Relax, for God loves you

RISE ABOVE

Good morning, my brothers and sisters. You know it's a good morning, for God created it. God is the Master of creation. He is marvelous in everything He does. My brothers and sisters, in everything that you go through, God wants you to rise above it. God doesn't want you to fall. He doesn't wish ill toward you. Look at it this way, you are going to come across people who are going to hate you, and throw negative vibes at you, but don't let that get you down. God doesn't want you to be down, but if you get down, He will uplift you.

Rise above your enemies
Rise above your mistakes
Rise above your downfalls
Rise above your faults
Rise above your lust
Rise above your impatience
Rise above demons
Above all, rise above Satan

SACRIFICE

Sacrifice yourself for the will of God
Sacrifice yourself for the honoring of God
Sacrifice yourself for the blessing of God
Sacrifice yourself for the riches of God
Sacrifice yourself for the kingdom of God
Sacrifice yourself for the glory of God
Sacrifice yourself for the uniqueness of God
Sacrifice yourself for just loving God

SATAN

Satan is a liar
Satan is a hater
Satan is a murderer
Satan is an adulterer
Satan is a destroyer
Satan is an accuser
Satan is an abuser
Satan is a loser

SAY GOODBYE

Say goodbye to fear
Say goodbye to doubt
Say goodbye to uncleanness
Say goodbye to anger
Say goodbye to that abusive relationship that you were in
Say goodbye to cigarettes
Say goodbye to drugs
Say goodbye to liquor and beer bottles
Say goodbye to that unfair job
Say goodbye to Satan

SEEK

Seek for God's righteousness
Seek for God's wisdom
Seek for God's knowledge
Seek for God's understanding
Seek for God's joy
Seek for God's power
Seek for God's help
Seek for God's strength
Seek for God's motivation
Seek for God's love
Seek for God's heart
Seek for God's kingdom

SERVE GOD

Serve God with fear
Serve God with compassion
Serve God with love
Serve God with obedience
Serve God with humbleness
Serve God with kindness
Serve God with faithfulness
Serve God with gentleness
Serve God with boldness
Serve God with all your might

SERVE GOD REGARDLESS

Serve God regardless of whether you get an expensive house
  or not
Serve God regardless of whether you get an expensive car or not
Serve God regardless of whether you get a high paying job or not
Serve God regardless of whether you are rich or poor
Serve God regardless of whether you get married or not
Serve God regardless of whether you get fancy clothes or not
Serve God regardless of whether you get noticed or not
Serve God for He has been good to you

SHAKE

God, shake depression from me
God, shake anger from me
God, shake sadness from me
God, shake misery from me
God, shake confusion from me
God, shake frustration from me
God, shake negativity from me
God, shake madness from me
God, shake lust from me
God, shake Satan from me

SHOW COMPASSION

Show compassion to your family
Show compassion to your friends
Show compassion to your neighbors
Show compassion to your church
Show compassion to everyone
Show compassion to Jesus Christ
Show compassion to God

STAND TALL II

Stand tall against your enemies
Stand tall against temptations
Stand tall in the day of battle
Stand tall in your tribulations
Stand tall in your trials
Stand tall in your faith
Stand tall in your firm beliefs
Stand tall in the storm
Stand tall with confidence
Stand tall with hope
Stand tall with joy
Stand tall with praises
Stand tall in yourself
Stand tall in the Word of God
Stand tall in Jesus Christ
Stand tall in the glory of God

STOP COMPLAINING

The problem with most of us Christians is that we complain all the time. Why do we complain? The Lord blesses us to wake up every morning, but we still complain. Think about when the Lord blesses you with a house and a car. Some people don't even have a place to stay, and yet you don't hear them complaining.

The Lord blesses you with food, so stop complaining
God blesses you with shelter, so stop complaining
The Lord blesses you with transportation, so stop complaining
God blesses you with rainy and sunny days, so stop complaining
The Lord gave you a wonderful family, so stop complaining
God blesses you to get an education, so stop complaining
The Lord blesses you to be successful, so stop complaining
God blesses you to be rich, so stop complaining
The Lord blesses you to be healthy, so stop complaining
God chose you to preach His holy Word, so stop complaining
The Lord blesses you to hear His Holy Word, so stop complaining
God blesses you to talk, so stop complaining
God blesses you to walk, so stop complaining
His Son died for our sins, so stop complaining
He made us joint heirs with Christ, so please stop complaining

STOP PLAYING GAMES

Stop playing games with each other's heart
Stop playing games with each other's mind
Stop playing games with each other's emotions
Stop playing games with yourselves
Stop playing games on your job
Stop playing games in the classroom
Stop playing games with people's money
Stop playing games in the church
Stop playing games with your family
Stop playing games with the Almighty God

STRIVE

Strive to be the best
Strive to pass the test
Strive to never fail
Strive to prevail
Strive to be on top
Strive to never stop
Strive to be good
Strive to be understood
Strive with hope
Strive with no joke
Strive with dignity
Strive with all your ability
Strive with faith
Strive with what it takes to make it to God

SUPPORT

Support your minister
Support your preacher
Support your bishop
Support your deacon
Support your evangelist
Support your usher
Support your choir director
Support your choir
Support your praise team
Support your brothers and sisters
Support your Bible class teacher
Support the Body of Christ

TELL GOD

Tell God that you love Him
Tell God that you want to be with Him
Tell God that you honor Him
Tell God that you adore Him
Tell God that you respect Him
Tell God that you will obey Him
Tell God thank You
Tell God you will bless Him

THANK YOU GOD

Thank You, God, for Your anointing
Thank You, God, for Your healing
Thank You, God, for feeding the poor
Thank You, God, for sheltering the homeless
Thank You, God, for lifting me up
Thank You, God, for Your protection
Thank You, God, for Your kindness
Thank You, God, for Your compassion
Thank You, God, for Your forgiveness
Thank You, God, for Your Son, Jesus Christ

THE ENEMY

The enemy does not want you to praise God
The enemy does not want you to love God
The enemy does not want you to worship God
The enemy does not want you to obey God
The enemy does not want you to honor God
The enemy does not want you to follow God
The enemy does not want you to please God
The enemy does not want you to seek God
The enemy does not want you to believe in God
And that enemy is Satan; the one I hate

THE GRACE OF GOD

The grace of God is peaceful
The grace of God is joyful
The grace of God is love
The grace of God is faithful
The grace of God is spectacular
The grace of God is marvelous
The grace of God is caring
The grace of God is sharing
The grace of God is eternal
The grace of God is Jesus Christ

THE ONE

The one you need to hate is Satan
The one you need to despise is Satan
The one you need to reject is Satan
The one you need to point the finger toward is Satan
The one you need to laugh at is Satan
The one you need to throw stones at is Satan
The one you need to rebuke is Satan

THE ONLY THING

The only thing I'm into doing is blessing God
The only thing I'm into doing is praising God
The only thing I'm into doing is following God
The only thing I'm into doing is relaxing with God
The only thing I'm into doing is worshiping God
The only thing I'm into doing is living with God
The only thing I'm into doing is loving God
The only thing I'm into doing is obeying God

THE POWER OF GOD

The power of God is amazing
The power of God is perfect
The power of God is mighty
The power of God is marvelous
The power of God is heroic
The power of God is tremendous
The power of God is unique
The power of God is justice
The power of God is wonderful
The power of God is full of greatness
The power of God is full of joy
The power of God is peace
The power of God is happiness
The power of God is pure love
The power of God is full of compassion

THE PRESENCE OF GOD

The presence of God is peaceful
The presence of God is joyful
The presence of God is wonderful
The presence of God is comfortable
The presence of God is powerful
The presence of God is unique
The presence of God is great
The presence of God is righteous
The presence of God is glorious
The presence of God is love

THE TRUTH SHALL SET YOU FREE

The truth shall set you free from hurt
The truth shall set you free from harm
The truth shall set you free from danger
The truth shall set you free from depression
The truth shall set you free from suicide
The truth shall set you free from murdering
The truth shall set you free from adultery
The truth shall set you free from sex addiction
The truth shall set you free from cocaine
The truth shall set you free from fibbing
The truth shall set you free from bondage

THE WILL OF GOD

The will of God is just
The will of God is perfect
The will of God is peace
The will of God is understanding
The will of God is joy
The will of God is marvelous
The will of God is tremendous
The will of God is amazing
The will of God is magnificent
The will of God is love

THE WRATH OF GOD

The wrath of God is nothing to play with
The wrath of God is powerful
The wrath of God is lethal
The wrath of God is judgement
The wrath of God is vital
The wrath of God is punishing
The wrath of God is brutal
The wrath of God is painful
The wrath of God is nothing that you want to experience

VICTORIOUS

At the end of the day, God will be victorious
At the end of the week, God will be victorious
At the end of the month, God will be victorious
At the end of the year, God will be victorious
At the end of the decade, God will be victorious
At the end of the century, God will be victorious
At the end of the millennium, God will be victorious
At the end of time, God will be victorious
At the end of the world, God will be victorious
At the end of the age, God will be victorious

WALK WITH ME

Though I may feel lonely, walk with me, God
Though I may sin, walk with me, God
Though I may feel weak, walk with me, God
Though I may cry, walk with me, God
Though I may feel empty, walk with me, God
Though I may feel discouraged, walk with me, God
Though I may feel guilty, walk with me, God
Though I may feel disappointed, walk with me, God
Walk with me, Lord, and never leave me.

WATCH OUT

Watch out for false prophets
Watch out for false teachers
Watch out for false witnesses
Watch out for deceivers
Watch out for adulterers
Watch out for crooked people
Watch out for hypocrites
Watch out for betrayers
Watch out for snakes
Watch out for the Anti Christ

WE ARE FREE

We are free to serve God
We are free to love God
We are free to honor God
We are free to obey God
We are free to praise God
We are free to acknowledge God
We are free to dwell with God
We are free to abide with God

WE BELONG

We belong to God
We belong to Jesus Christ
We belong to the Holy Spirit
We belong to heaven

WELCOME GOD

Welcome God into your home
Welcome God into your education
Welcome God on your jobs
Welcome God into your mind
Welcome God into your conversation
Welcome God everywhere you go

WHAT ABOUT ME?

I am the One who wakes you up in the morning
I am the One who comforts you
I am the One who truly loves you
I am the One who uplifts you
I am the One who encourages you
I am the One who blesses you
I am the One who heals you
I am the One who strengthens you
I am the One who holds you
I am the One who recognizes you
I am the One who created you
So, what about me? Says the Lord God

WHATEVER GOD'S HEART DESIRE

Whatever God's heart desires, you should do
Whatever God's heart desires, you should take heed to
Whatever God's heart desires, you should obey
Whatever God's heart desires, you should jump to
Whatever God's heart desires, you should care for
Whatever God's heart desires, you should be willing to die for
Whatever God's heart desires, you should count it all joy

WHY NOT!

Why not serve God!
Why not bless God!
Why not honor God!
Why not obey God!
Why not praise God!
Why not trust God!
Why not have faith in God!
Why not believe in God!
Why not love God!

WITH FAITH

With faith, you can move mountains
With faith, you can knock down walls
With faith, you can achieve your goals
With faith, you can stand up to the enemy
With faith, you can overcome obstacles
With faith, you can love
With faith, you can overcome fear
With faith, you can please God (Hebrews 11:6)

WITH GOD

With God, there is life
With God, there is peace
With God, there is joy
With God, there is love
With God, there is boldness
With God, there is power
With God, there is praise
With God, there is happiness
With God, there is grace
With God, there is mercy
With God, there is comfort
With God, there is Jesus Christ
With God, there is the Holy Spirit
With God, there is everything

YOU ARE BETTER OFF

You are better off serving God
You are better off following Jesus Christ
You are better off praying
You are better off reading the Bible
You are better off getting knowledge
You are better off getting understanding
You are better off getting wisdom
You are better off loving others
You are better off going to heaven

YOU DID

Holy Trinity, You did a great job creating the universe
Holy Trinity, You did a great job creating man
Holy Trinity, You did a great job creating woman
Holy Trinity, You did a great job creating animals
Holy Trinity, You did a great job creating nature
Holy Trinity, You did a great job creating heavenly angels
Holy Trinity, You did a great job creating heaven
Holy Trinity, You did a great job creating everything

ABOUT THE AUTHOR

Demetrice M. Gates was born January 3, 1979 at Grady Memorial Hospital located in Atlanta, Georgia. For 13 years, He lived in a rough and violent environment, particularly in the inner city ghetto of Atlanta. Then, after the death of his father, he, along with his family, relocated to College Park, Georgia where he attended and graduated from Benjamin E. Banneker High School. Demetrice is a proud member of Holiness, Spiritual, and Truth Church, which is led by his mother, Elder Betty Gates. Demetrice loves people, and loves to encourage them. He believes that God is the inspiration and motivation for everything. With the gift that God granted to him, he desires to touch the world.